THE ARCHAEOLOGY OF MANCHESTER IN 20 DIGS

Michael Nevell

AMBERLEY

First published 2020

Amberley Publishing
The Hill, Stroud
Gloucestershire, GL5 4EP

www.amberley-books.com

British Library Cataloguing in Publication Data.
A catalogue record for this book is available from the British Library.

ISBN 978 1 4456 9428 3 (print)
ISBN 978 1 4456 9429 0 (ebook)

Typesetting by Aura Technology and Software Services, India.
Printed in Great Britain.

Contents

Introduction

Manchester is one of the great industrial cities of the nineteenth century, the world centre for cotton yarn production and marketing until the mid-twentieth century, both of which have left a legacy of hundreds of industrial mills and warehouses. It was home to both new forms of capitalist production and new forms of democratic organisation in the form of trade unions. It saw the opening of the first industrial arterial canal in Britain (the Bridgewater Canal) in 1761 and the first intercity passenger railway, the Liverpool to Manchester line, in 1830. It was also notorious as the 'shock city' of the nineteenth century. Those who visited it during the middle decades of the century were astounded or, like the social and political commentator Frederick Engels, more often horrified by the city's industrial face. Hundreds of cotton factories and chimneys, the narrow alleyways and overcrowded houses, were packed into the present twenty-first-century city centre.

Yet Manchester's story is more than just that of the Industrial Revolution and its consequences. The Victorian civic authorities celebrated the Roman foundation of the city as a fort and civilian settlement, confidently ascribed to the general and governor of Britannia, Gnaeus Julius Agricola, in AD 79. The city does have Roman roots in Castlefield, though whether General Agricola ever visited is doubtful. But the landscape of the city is much older as excavation ahead of the building of Manchester Airport's second runway in the late 1990s demonstrated with the uncovering of the homes of the first farmers in the region, from over 5,000 years ago. Nor were the Romans entering an empty landscape in the mid-first century AD. Increasingly, archaeology is identifying more and more late prehistoric farmsteads dotted along the river valleys of the city region: the Bollin, Irwell, and Medlock.

After the Romans a new landscape of small agricultural communities emerged in the medieval period, the origin of many of the suburbs of the twenty-first-century city such as Baguley, Chorlton, Moston, Northenden and Wythenshawe. In 1500 Manchester was a modest town, one of thirty-four market centres in the North West. It grew slowly in the Tudor and Stuart periods, doubling its population in the century between 1563 and 1664. Thereafter, it expanded rapidly; between 1664 and 1773 the population increased sevenfold to *c.* 23,000. Then it exploded, trebling in the space of a generation to reach 75,281 by 1801. In that year, there were thirty-three textile mills in the city, where there had been none in 1773, and by 1851 this number had risen to more than 100 and the city's population had reached 303,382. The city and its region of *c.* 1.2 million people and

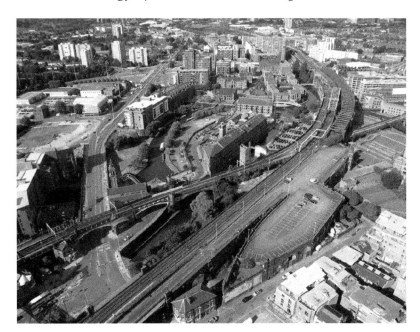

Roman and industrial Castlefield as seen from Beetham Tower in 2008. (Image courtesy of the Greater Manchester Archaeological Advisory Service)

more than 1,000 textile mills had, in the space of just seventy-eight years (1773–1851), become one of the largest urban centres in Europe. Such rapid industrialization has left a great variety of above- and below-ground remains in the city which, coupled with the detailed archaeological investigations recorded in this book, provide a model for charting industrial urbanization in other mercantile cities.

Manchester has always had the ability to reinvent itself: as an Elizabethan linen market town; then as a Georgian weaving and market centre for fustian cloth; then as the world's largest cotton spinning town. When the expansion of the textile industry in the mid-nineteenth century slowed, Manchester was reinvented as a Victorian commercial and engineering centre and international shipping port. Though badly affected by economic decline in the 1960s and 1970s, and the loss of traditional industries such as coal mining, engineering, transport, and textiles, Manchester set about reinventing itself as an education, music and sports destination on the back of extensive urban regeneration and renewal. Significantly for the current book, in the late twentieth century the city reinvented itself as a pioneer of heritage-led urban regeneration with schemes around the medieval cathedral quarter and the Roman and industrial quarter of Castlefield, both of which were linked to a rejuvenated public transport network. The opening of the Metrolink tram service in 1992 allowed fast access to the city centre.

The year 2020 marks forty years since the first professional archaeological unit was founded in Manchester. It seems appropriate, then, to review the emerging understanding of the city's archaeology and history through twenty of the most significant excavations undertaken. This is, of course, a personal choice but I have endeavoured to select those sites that represent the full chronological development of the city as we understand it in the early twenty-first century, as well as sites which marked significant shifts in either our understanding of the city's development or in the way its archaeology and history was managed.

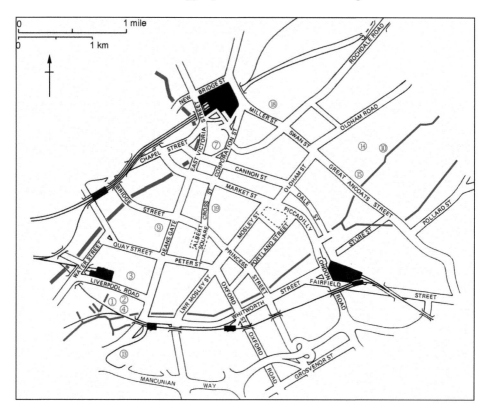

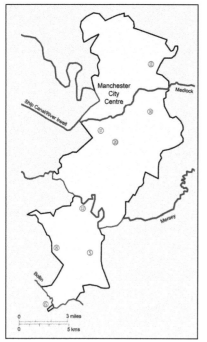

Above: Map of central Manchester showing dig sites mentioned in this book. Numbers refer to the dig sections.

Left: Map of the city of Manchester showing the location of digs outside the city centre discussed in this book. Numbers refer to the dig sections.

Dig 1

Manchester's First Archaeologist – Bruton at Roman Manchester (1906–7)

'It is not every great City that is able – by merely peeling off the accumulations of centuries – to expose to view under the very shadow of its railway viaducts and amid the roar of its traffic the relics of a vanished Empire' (Bruton, 1909). In this way Manchester's first modern archaeologist, Dr Francis Archibald Bruton (1860–1930), introduced his account of the excavations of the remains of the Roman fort at Castlefield. He also neatly summarised some of the problems and challenges of excavating a large industrial city such as Manchester.

Bruton was not a professional archaeologist, but rather a naturalist and, at the time of the dig, an assistant master at Manchester Grammar School, teaching engineering and science subjects (Graham & Phythian, 1965, 100–101). He was a member of many local societies, including the Lancashire and Cheshire Antiquarian Society, on whose committee he served from 1910 to 1920; and a founding member of the Manchester branch of the Classical Association in 1904. This interest in the past led him to help excavate other Roman forts through the Classical Association: Melandra Castle in 1905, Castleshaw in 1907 and 1908 (Walker, 1989, 6–7) and Caer Llugwy near Conwy in the years 1920 to 1922 (Bruton & Hall, 1923). After the First World War he compiled a centenary volume for the 100th anniversary of the Peterloo massacre in 1919, recording eyewitness accounts of that momentous day, and wrote an introductory history of Manchester and Salford and a volume on the landscape and history of Lancashire.

For his era Bruton kept detailed archaeological records, used photography extensively and had an eye for unpicking the various phases of activity on a site – probably reflecting his scientific background. Although altars, Roman glass and pottery, and stone foundations had been recorded from within and around the fort during the building of the Bridgewater Canal in the 1760s and a railway line during the 1840s, systematic work had not been undertaken. Thus, Bruton can properly be said to have led the first scientific exploration of Roman Manchester. During the years 1906 and 1907 his team undertook the first large-scale excavations of the interior of the Roman fort at Manchester.

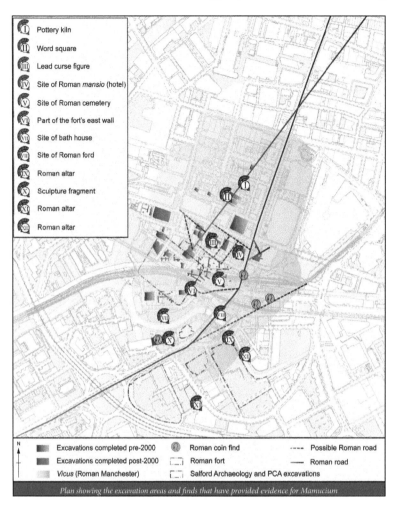

I	Pottery kiln
II	Word square
III	Lead curse figure
IV	Site of Roman *mansio* (hotel)
V	Site of Roman cemetery
VI	Part of the fort's east wall
VII	Site of bath house
VIII	Site of Roman ford
IX	Roman altar
X	Sculpture fragment
XI	Roman altar
XII	Roman altar

N

■ Excavations completed pre-2000	◎ Roman coin find
■ Excavations completed post-2000	⬚ Roman fort
▨ *Vicus* (Roman Manchester)	⬚ Salford Archaeology and PCA excavations

---- Possible Roman road
—— Roman road

Plan showing the excavation areas and finds that have provided evidence for Mamucium

A map of Roman Manchester showing dig sites, roads and key finds as we understand it in the early twenty-first century.

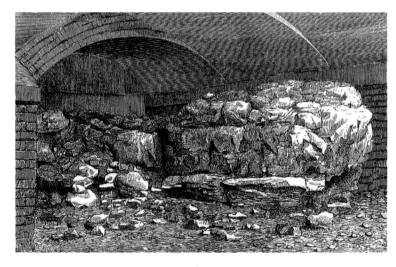

The remains of the eastern gateway at the Roman fort in Manchester in the late nineteenth century, beneath railway arch number 95 in Castlefield.

Bruton's work in 1906 focussed on the north-western corner of the fort, on a site bounded by Duke Street and Duke Place (Jones & Grealey, 1974, 18). Here he opened a large trench, 25 metres by 30. This identified the line of the western stone wall of the fort, and an earlier turf and timber rampart, fronted by two ditches, and substantial internal features. The internal features included two parallel roads running north to

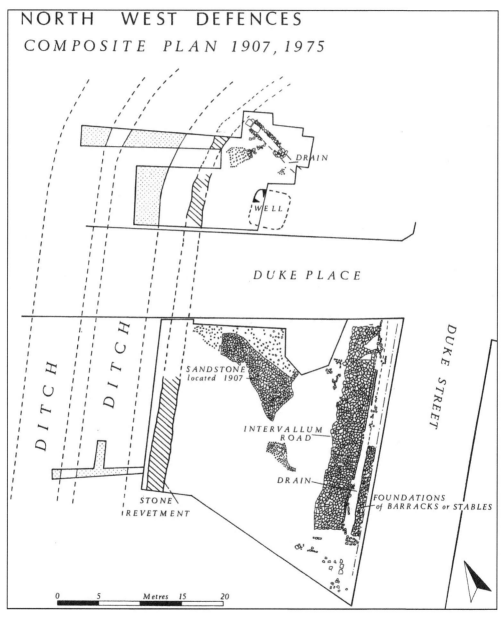

Plan of Dr Bruton's excavations at Duke Place in 1907. (Image courtesy of the Greater Manchester Archaeological Advisory Service)

south, one containing a well-preserved stone drain in the centre (Jones & Grealey, 1974, 18–19). Around 50 feet (30 metres) within the western defences of the fort were a series of sandstone blocks set in clay running north to south but beneath the later, eastern, Roman road. This substantial building was located again in 1975 and once more in 2005 at Duke's Place and interpreted as a granary building (Walker, 1986, 14–15; Gregory, 2008).

His research in 1907 explored the eastern interior of the fort, although it was not possible to open large areas. Bruton was able to sink four trial trenches in a timber yard inside the eastern defences behind Collier Street. These trenches failed to find any intact Roman deposits. However, that same year his team dug a trench along the line of the eastern defences, by the side of the only standing stone fragment of the defensive wall. This work indicated that the defences in this area comprised a solid stone rampart 2.1–2.75 metres thick, lying on natural gravels, mirroring the western defences (Jones & Grealey, 1974, 18–19). It was nearly 100 years before this could be confirmed by further trenching in the eastern part of the fort in 2005 (Gregory, 2007a).

Dr Bruton's legacy was to confirm the overall size of the auxiliary Roman fort, roughly 160 metres (175 yards) from west to east and 128 metres (140 yards) from north to south, and to establish that there were several phases of activity, including a major rebuilding phase in stone. The Roman fort's interior was investigated only sporadically throughout the rest of the twentieth century until the opportunity for a further major excavation arose in 1979 (see below, Dig 4).

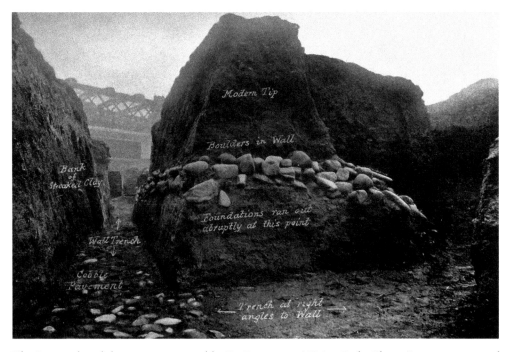

The Roman fort defences, as excavated by Dr Bruton on 1906 at Duke Place. (Image courtesy of the Greater Manchester Archaeological Advisory Service)

Dig 2

The Deansgate Dig – The Beginnings of Community Archaeology (1972)

There is a long tradition of archaeological study and investigation within the City of Manchester. From the early twentieth century the University of Manchester has been at the forefront of this research, through the work of a succession of lecturers in history and curators based within the Manchester Museum, and from 1969 through the Archaeology Department. The Deansgate Dig of 1972, which explored the Roman settlement to the north of the fort, was an important moment in the development of modern archaeological research within the city. Not only did it demonstrate the survival of extensive Roman and nineteenth-century archaeology deposits within the city centre, just a few centimetres below the current ground level, but it was also the first modern community excavation in Manchester, involving

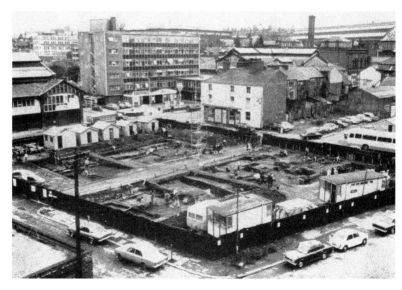

The Deansgate dig, 1972. Led by Prof Barri Jones of the University of Manchester Archaeology Department, this was the first community dig within the city. It also demonstrated the survival of substantial Roman archaeology in the Castlefield area of the city.

hundreds of individuals young and old, revived interest in Manchester's Roman past and led to the creation of Britain's first urban heritage park.

The dig was led by Professor Barri Jones, the first professor of archaeology appointed by the University of Manchester and a classically trained archaeologist with an interest in the Roman army. As Martin Biddle, at the time chairman of RESCUE, aptly put it the success of the dig was down in large measure to 'his skills both as an archaeologist and a teacher', (Jones & Grealey, 1974, vii). In the early 1970s the archaeology department at the university was small, with just four full-time lecturers supported by the staff at Manchester Museum, also based at the university and home to the dig archive from Bruton's earlier investigations of Roman Manchester. Professional archaeology in Britain was in its infancy, with just a few hundred full-time posts outside the university sector, though those numbers were rapidly growing as the need to record archaeology ahead of new infrastructure and housing projects rapidly increased. However, there was as yet no professional unit based within the Manchester city region so it was left to Professor Jones to raise funds and the awareness of the importance of, and need for, archaeological work ahead of redevelopment within Manchester. Thus, the Deansgate Dig was a major milestone in raising awareness nationally about the increasing threat of redevelopment to archaeology within the historic centres of northern industrial cities (Jones, 1984, 23–5).

This excavation recovered, for the first time, extensive evidence for the Roman vicus, the civilian settlement attached to the fort. Previous work in Castlefield had hinted at settlement beyond the walls of the auxiliary Roman fort, focussed on the Medlock river crossing at the southern end of Deansgate, east of the fort. It was the Deansgate Dig that showed that there was a large civilian settlement extending to the north of the fort.

The Deansgate Dig of 1972 lay on the southern side of Liverpool Road, west of the White Lion Pub, in an area now laid out as part of the Roman Gardens (Jones & Grealey, 1974). Although open fields in the early nineteenth century, workers' houses were built over the area in the 1810s and 1820s when the grid of streets formed by Barton Street, Beaufort Street, Bridgewater Street, Canal Street, Collier Street, Duke Place, Duke Street, Manor Street, Robert Street, Southern Street, White Lion Street and Worsley Street was laid out.

The earliest activity took the form of a series of ditches and palisades to the west of a wide cobbled road running from the northern gateway of the fort, representing early military activity, probably a defended annex to the first fort. These features were abandoned within a few years and backfilled with building rubble such as wattle and daub. A series of small timber buildings were then built either side of the road, some with back yards. There were several phases. In the early second century, there were three buildings, no more than 5 metres by 6 metres, including an open-sided shed with a smithing hearth. In the later second century these buildings were replaced by three larger timber structures, 12.5 metres by 5 metres and 10 metres by 10 metres in size, and a third that contained a further furnace. To the north and west of these buildings was a large group of thirty iron smithing hearths of a similar date, whose use ran into the third century.

The date range of the pottery from the dig suggested initial intense activity beginning in the later AD 70s and continuing down to the end of the second century. Third-century industrial activity was extensive until the middle of the century, after which settlement in this part of the vicus appears to have ceased. In the early second century most of the pottery types came from local sources, general Cheshire Plains Wares from the kilns at Northwich and Wilderspool and pots manufactured at the kilns at Holt in

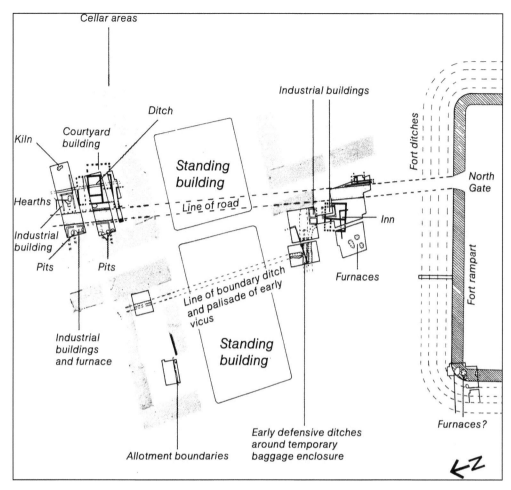

Plan of the Roman excavations undertaken by Prof Barri Jones on the Roman vicus at Manchester from 1972 to 1978.

western Cheshire. Fabrics from further afield were confined to Black Burnished wares types 1 and 2 from the mid-second century onwards, amphora from Spain and Samian ware from southern and central France. Colour-coated fabrics from the Nene Valley and Severn Valley appear from the late second century onwards. A late fourth-century pottery fragment from a drain linked to the penultimate road surface immediately north of the gateway showed activity continuing around the fort into this late Roman period.

Although the Deansgate Dig failed to reveal any evidence for post-Roman activity, it is notable for one further aspect. This was the first time that industrial workers' housing was excavated in Manchester, indeed one of the first occasions in Britain when the houses of nineteenth-century industrial Britain were excavated using contemporary archaeological techniques. The fact that the same recording techniques were used to recover data about the nineteenth-century archaeology of the houses along White Lion Street, as for the Roman levels, foreshadowed the twenty-first-century archaeological research on workers' housing within the city.

Dig 3

Manchester and Early Christianity – The Manchester Wordsquare (1978)

Proposals in the mid-1970s to build new houses in Castlefield brought Professor Jones and his team from the University of Manchester back to the area to conduct further rescue excavations. Finance remained a problem and a mixture of volunteers (the newly formed Greater Manchester Group) and, later, professionals funded by the Department of the Environment, Greater Manchester County and the Manpower Services Commission supported the digs from November 1977 to August 1978. A series of sites were excavated in the Byrom Street and St John Street area north of Liverpool Road and approximately 110 metres north of the Roman fort (Gregory, 2007a; Jones & Reynolds, 1978, 5). Here, further extensive remains of the civilian settlement were located, proving that it was much bigger than the fort site, and one find in particular that would attract international attention.

The earliest activity in the Byrom Street area was represented by a ditch located in a trench 40 metres west of the main 1977–78 excavation. This ditch had a similar profile and alignment to one seen in 1972. The extent and position of this ditch suggests it was part of the defended annex of the earliest fort (Gregory, 2007a, 181–2; Jones & Reynolds, 1978, 7). This was associated with the continuation of the roadway leading from the northern gate of the fort first seen in the Deansgate Dig of 1972. The road was well used, just as had been recorded on the 1972 site. Excavations showed successive rebuilds and resurfacing, with evidence for gravel quarry pits for its construction. In places the road foundations survived up to *c.* 0.7 metres deep and a width of at least 6 metres (Jones & Reynolds, 1978, 7–8).

The main Byrom Street and St John Street sites contained the remains of fifteen Roman buildings, spanning the late first century to the early third century. Most of the buildings were sited immediately alongside the road. In the late first and early second century, six small timber buildings were built, the largest being 7.2 metres by 4 metres (Building Q) on the eastern side of the road. This was probably a blacksmith's workshop with a hearth and working area producing iron nails. Further smithing hearths were excavated behind the buildings on the western side of the road (Jones & Reynolds, 1978, 7–9).

Another form of industrial activity in the vicus was represented by a pottery kiln found around 25 metres east of the road. This kiln comprised a circular stone-lined chamber,

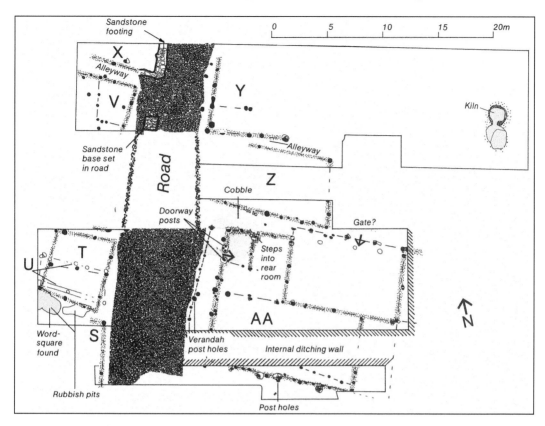

A plan of the Byrom Street excavations undertaken by Prof Barri Jones in 1977 and 1978, showing the second-century AD Roman buildings and road. The location of the rubbish pit containing the Manchester Wordsquare is shaded yellow.

1.1 metres wide and 0.4 metres deep with remains of the internal pedestal surviving, fronted by a firing area that was largely taken up by a pit for the rakings of ash and charcoal (Jones & Reynolds, 1978, 9–11). Several distorted fragments of pottery, wasters from the last firing of the kiln, were excavated from the chamber. The pottery produced, grey-brown jars, was similar to Cheshire Plains Ware type products seen at kilns from Middlewich, Northwich and Wilderspool. This is the only Roman pottery kiln yet discovered in Manchester and appears to date from the mid-second century. Elsewhere, the style and date range of the 30,000 pottery sherds excavated was very similar to that seen on the 1972 Deansgate Dig site.

In the later second century these buildings were replaced by larger post-built structures. The biggest was Building AA, a winged timber structure on the eastern side of the road 13.5 metres deep and 18.1 metres wide, with a verandah fronting the road. It also had an internal courtyard 10.1 metres by 6.6 metres. This building was in use into the mid-third century and possibly later. West of the road, three smaller timber buildings were built in the late second century, including one with a verandah on a sandstone base that encroached on to the road (Building X) (Jones & Reynolds, 1978, 12–13).

The evidence for an early military annex and a pottery kiln added significantly to our understanding of the vicus, its size and its function. However, the most startling

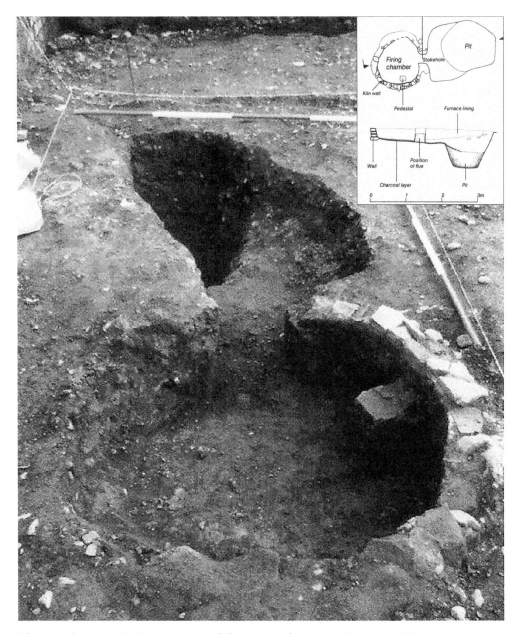

The second-century AD Roman pottery kiln excavated at Byrom Street in 1978.

discovery from the dig was a single sherd of discarded amphora found in a rubbish pit dating to the third quarter of the second century. Discovered by one of the volunteers, Craig Brisbane, in a pit truncated by the construction of Building T on the western side of the road, its significance was not at first realised as it was one of several sherds from the pit and all needed cleaning. It wasn't the Spanish pottery fabric that was the surprise, it was the graffito scratched into its surface that received international attention.

Cut into the shoulder of the amphora fragment were three incomplete lines of text that bore the letters 'ROTAS OPERA TEN'. When complete they would have read as follows:

ROTAS
OPERA
TENET
AREPO
SATOR

This palindrome (a piece of text that reads identically backwards or when read up or down) can be translated as 'Arepo the sower guides the wheels with care', seemingly nonsense. There is a suggestion that it can be associated with the Stoic philosophy movement. However, remove the repeated 'A' and 'O', or alpha and omega, and we have an anagram of the Latin words PATER NOSTER, the first two words of the Christian prayer 'Our Father'. The alpha and omega also have Christian connections. Eleven inscriptions like this, always as graffiti, are known from the Roman Empire before AD 500 and were probably used to identify fellow believers at a time when the Christian religion was outlawed and being persecuted by the Roman authorities. Other word games are known across the empire and it is likely that this wordsquare was an adaptation of a form already in common circulation (Gregory, 2007b, 133–136).

The discovery of the Manchester Wordsquare, this Christian word puzzle, was an international sensation. It made headlines in the Vatican newspaper at the time of its discovery as one of the oldest pieces of evidence for Christianity in Britain. According to the Christian writer Tertullian, Christianity did not reach Britain until the late second century. It would be AD 260 before the Christian religion was recognised as legitimate and not until AD 313 did it become the official religion of the empire. Yet in Britain it is clear that Christian belief was well established before the fourth century (Jones & Mattingly, 1990, 295–300). The Manchester Wordsquare remains one of the earliest examples of Christianity yet found in Roman Britain, and one of the few associated with a military site before the fourth century.

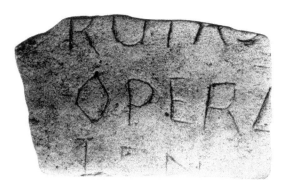 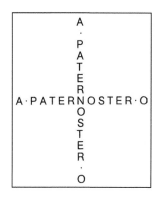

Above: The Manchester Wordsquare, scratched on a fragment of Spanish amphora and found in a late second-century rubbish pit in the northern vicus.

Above right: A decoding of the Christian Wordsquare, spelling out the first two letters of the Lord's Prayer.

Dig 4

The Northgate Roman Dig (1979–81)

With the open areas in Castlefield rapidly disappearing due to redevelopment, in May 1979 an opportunity arose to excavate the site of the northern gateway of the Roman fort, immediately south of the 1972 Deansgate Dig, between Manor Street and Bridgewater Street. Once more Professor Jones put together a dig team of volunteers and professionals to excavate this area, partly funded through the Manpower Services Commission. In that same year the City Council established the Castlefield Conservation Area and published a document, entitled *Historic Castlefield*, which called for the retention and restoration of the canals and surviving historic buildings within the area, including Liverpool Road station and Higher Campfield Market. The dig and this strategy document ultimately led to the establishment of Britain's first urban heritage park, opened in 1982, to display the industrial and Roman remains of the area, including the northern gateway of the fort and the associated Roman settlement excavated in 1972 and 1979 to 1981 (Nevell, 2019a, 109; Parkinson-Bailey, 2000, 215).

As excavation work continued sporadically throughout 1980, negotiations with the Greater Manchester Council also proceeded about funding archaeology in the county on a more permanent basis. The conclusion of these negotiations was the establishment of the Greater Manchester Archaeology Unit, to be based at Manchester University but with core funding from the Greater Manchester Council, on 1 September 1980. Additional project funding was raised from the Manpower Services Commission and the newly established unit immediately took over the Northgate excavations and the core professional team of dig supervisors previously employed by Professor Jones. This was a pivotal moment: the establishment of the city's first professional archaeology unit with a link to the local university, a formula that remains the basis for overseeing professional archaeological work within Greater Manchester in the third decade of the twenty-first century (GMAU, 1981, 3–4; Nevell, 2019a, 109).

In 1979 the hopes of locating anything other than fragmentary remains associated with the northern fort defences were low. Small-scale excavations were carried out across these defences in the early twentieth century by Phelps (in 1912), in the 1950s by Petch (in the years 1950–1, 1954 and 1956), and in the years 1965–67 by J. H. Williams (Jones & Grealey, 1974, 23–7). These excavations were located in the area between Beaufort Street, Duke Street and Collier Street and, although fragmentary and with a high level of truncation by later activity, helped to establish the line of the northern

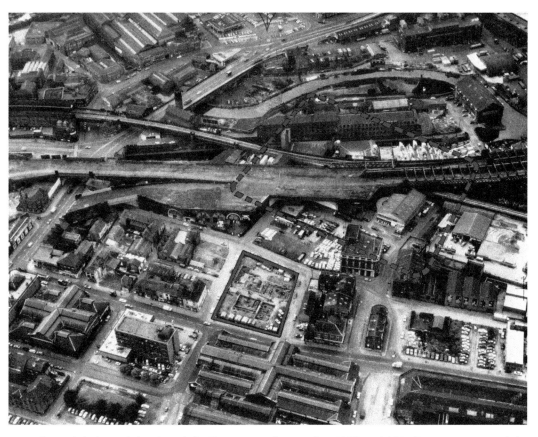

An aerial view of the site of the Roman north gate dig, 1979 to 1981. (Image courtesy of the Greater Manchester Archaeological Advisory Service)

wall of the Roman fort as well as providing information on its ditches and the probable location of the northern gateway (Walker, 1986, 21–60). Professor Jones's work in 1979 and 1980 established not only the location and form of the northern gateway, but also confirmed there were significant remains associated with it. From September 1980 to autumn 1981 these exploratory investigations were expanded into a large, open area excavation, similar in size to the 1972 Deansgate Dig. The excavation site, 29 metres by 41 metres, straddled the northern defences, encompassing the intervallum road, the rampart, fort wall and northern gateway, the ditches and, beyond these, a small area of the external settlement.

Five phases of Roman activity were identified, encompassing 6,000 objects and over 1,000 Roman deposits, spanning the full chronological history of the Roman fort. The earliest activity on the site was the Phase 1 timber fort, built in the late AD 70s. A 13-metre length of rampart was excavated, surviving no more than 0.8 metres in height. The rampart was built directly onto the sands and gravels of the local geology, with a base of narrow timber planks, around 0.15 metres in diameter, laid transversely giving a base 6–8 metres in width. The core was revetted by a single vertical stack of turfs placed over the timber foundations. It is likely that the rampart was 3–4 metres in

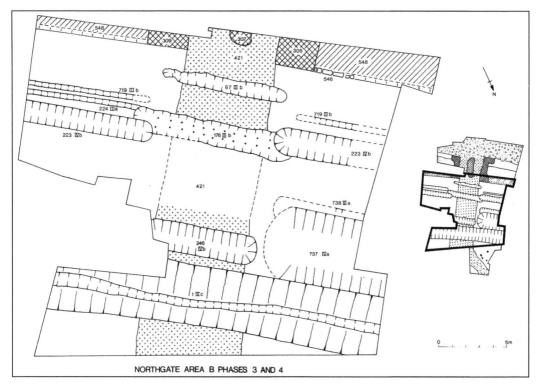

NORTHGATE AREA B PHASES 3 AND 4

A plan of the Phase Three defences, *c.* AD 200, at the north gate dig site. (Image courtesy of the Greater Manchester Archaeological Advisory Service)

height, with a patrol walkway. The original northern gateway was built in timber with two square timber towers flanking a double-portal entrance 4 metres wide. In front of the gateway was a single ditch, crossed by the northern exit road, at this date 6.5 metres wide and constructed from the local gravel. This road was located by Professor Jones in 1978, 1977 and in 1972.

In the second phase of Roman Manchester's life, from approximately AD 90 to roughly AD 160, the timber and earth fort was improved, the rampart strengthened and the northern gateway replaced. To the north of the fort, buildings and iron furnaces were constructed in the vicus, which now expanded over the annexe ditches to the north-west and north-east but was probably defended by its own ditch and palisade. This period of occupation ended with demolition of the fort, involving slighting of the rampart, burning of the northern gateway and possibly the abandonment of the northern vicus. The destruction of the fort may have been due to the redeployment of its garrison further to the north, following the decision of the emperor Antoninus Pius in the AD 140s to occupy southern Scotland (Walker, 1986, 35–38).

Roman Manchester reached its peak in the late second century, around AD 160 to around AD 200, Phase 3 of the Northgate site. Around AD 160 a new timber fort, 0.9 ha larger than its predecessors, was built with a double ditch defensive system and a freshly resurfaced exit road. Evidence for this third timber fort was excavated by both

Bruton and Jones at Duke Place in 1907 and 1975. Sometime during this phase access to the northern gateway was blocked by the digging of shallow ditch revetted by stakes across the width of the exit road. Precisely how this should be interpreted is unclear.

At the beginning of Phase 4, around AD 200, the third timber fort was demolished and a new fort built entirely in stone: gateways, walls and interior buildings. It is this fort that has left what the historian A. J. P. Taylor called the 'least interesting Roman remain in England': the inner rubble core of the eastern gateway, which lies beneath a railway arch behind Collier Street. The form of the northern gateway, and probably that of the eastern one too, was a two-arched stone tower, 7.3 metres wide and *c.* 11 m wide. Bearing in mind the extensive nineteenth-century disturbance across the fort, one of the more surprising finds from this phase of activity was the survival in situ of a few of the lowest course of wall facing stones immediately north of the gateway. Behind the rampart, and also built during this phase, was an intervallum road around 4 metres wide. This fort is also probably to be associated with a fragment of monumental inscription found within the fort in 1832 that records building work during the reign of Septimius Severus and his son, Geta, during the years AD 198 and AD 209 (Roman Inscriptions of Britain No. 581).

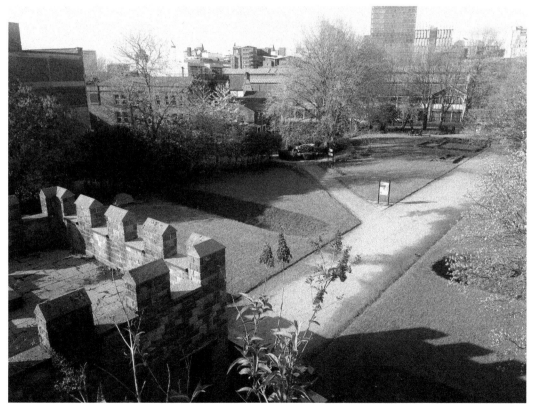

The reconstructed Manchester north gate and the fort defences and road beyond, set out as the Roman Gardens park. This area is part of the Manchester Urban Heritage Park established in the early 1980s as part of the regeneration of the Castlefield area.

This was probably undertaken by a detachment of Raetians and Noricans from the Second Legion Italica, recorded on two inscribed stones found elsewhere in the fort (Roman Inscriptions of Britain No. 576).

During this phase, probably in the late third century, a new road was built north of the gateway. This was about 3.5 metres wide and led in a northward direction from the eastern side of the exit road. It has been suggested this road was constructed to bring supplies from the River Irwell to the fort in the later Roman period (Walker, 1986, 50–1). By the fourth century, a large outer ditch had been dug beyond the fort's existing ditch system, cutting through the exit road. This seems to have coincided with the blocking of the northern gateway, suggesting that the exit roadway and vicus had both fallen out of use. The double ditch system remained in use, with later fourth-century pottery and two late fourth-century coins being recovered from the ditch fills.

Phase five activity, which most postdate the late fourth century, comprises a series of four pits dug across the exit road and into the top or the inner defensive ditch. In the absence of artefacts and radio-carbon dates it's very difficult to interpret these features. It has been suggested that they might be sunken-floored buildings from the early medieval period (Walker, 1986, 53–54). More recently, it has been suggested that they might represent a refortification of the Manchester fort associated with the Saxon reconquest of the area from the Danes in the early tenth century (Griffiths, 2001). However, no evidence of refortification in the early tenth century was found during the excavations through the eastern fort defences in 2005 and in the absence of secure dating and artefacts they must remain an enigma. These features may have been very short lived and were sealed by a sandstone rubble representing the collapse of the northern gateway and walls sometime in Phase Six (Walker, 1986, 54–55).

Dig 5

Peel Hall, Wythenshawe (1981)

The first modern archaeological dig to explore a site outside the city centre took place in 1981 and 1982 on the site of the moated Peel Hall in Wythenshawe and was led by the newly formed Greater Manchester Archaeological Unit. The excavations focussed upon the moated platform in response to a proposed scheme of works by Manchester City Council which included clearing the moat and laying out the site of the farmhouse. The site lay in the old manor of Etchells.

By the late medieval period, the fourteenth and fifteenth centuries, what was later to become the city of Manchester had been divided into a network of small manors, each with its own manor house and farmsteads (some even with their own moat, hunting grounds and corn mills). Most of these later medieval manors and the evidence for the late medieval economy have long since been built over and lost. However, there are some notable survivals within the city boundaries: the timber-framed fourteenth-century Baguley Hall and the sixteenth-century timber hall at Clayton and several manor sites that have not been built upon and might contain below-ground remains, such as the site of Moston Hall and the moated Peel Hall in Wythenshawe.

The site of the medieval Peel Hall in Wythenshawe, still surrounded by its water-filled moat and accessed via a seventeenth-century stone bridge. This was the first site excavated outside the city centre by the newly formed Greater Manchester Archaeological Unit.

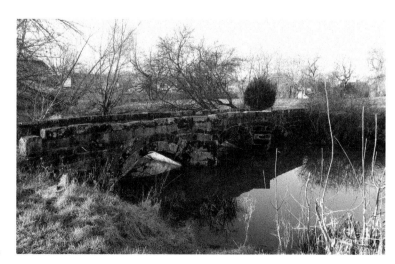

Peel Hall, being on council land in Wythenshawe Park, was an ideal site to begin investigation into the ancient halls of the county. A Manpower Services Scheme was set up in 1981 to excavate the moated platforms at Peel Hall before the council restoration works began. GMAU established the 'Country Houses of Greater Manchester' project in 1982 to better understand the results of the excavations at Peel Hall, and three other hall sites excavated in 1981 and 1982: Denton Hall and Dukinfield Hall in Tameside and Peel Hall in Wigan (Walker & Tindall, 1985, 33–43).

The Arderne family are recorded as owners of the manor in the fourteenth century and obtained a licence for a chapel at the manor of Etchells, probably at Peel Hall, in 1360. The manor passed to the Stanley family in 1408 and may have been the family seat. During the sixteenth century it changed hands on several occasions. The earliest known occurrence of the name Peel dates from 1519, when there is a reference to 'the Pele of Echellys' (Dodgson, 1970, 241). In 1557 the manor and hall were acquired by the Tatton family, who repaired the building for use as a dower house (Earwaker, 1877, 276–8). A survey of 1648 specifically mentions 'The House and gardens within the mote, the outhouses gardens and Coorte without the Mote' (John Rylands University Library, Manchester, TWY/195). From the end of the 1690s the manor house was leased to tenant farmers (Groves, 1994, 15). Peel Hall was demolished around 1809 and replaced by a T-shaped, brick-built farmhouse of two and three storeys, itself demolished in 1976.

The moated platform at Peel Hall is around 31 metres by around 33 metres, encompassing an area of roughly 2,700 square meters, surrounded by a water-filled moat around 10 metres to around 16 metres wide and accessed by a three-arched stone bridge from the seventeenth century. Four trenches, A, B, C, and D, covering an area of 150 square meters were excavated. One was placed in the south-west corner of the platform over the site of the farmhouse demolished in the 1970s (Trench D), a second (Trench A) to the north of this. The other two were located on the eastern side of the platform, to the north and south of the bridge (Trench B and Trench C).

Two successive cobbled surfaces were located in Trench A to the north of the farmhouse, both with a bedding layer of sand. This cobbling coincides with the position of the access road to the farmhouse shown on OS mapping from 1872 onwards. A sondage dug on the south side of Trench A provides possibly the best indication of the stratigraphical development of the site. Below the turf and dark brown loam topsoil was an orange brown clay, which overlay a yellow clay. This last layer in turn scaled a dark grey loam, which is said to have contained eighteenth and nineteenth-century pottery, along with inclusions of stone and brick. This loam layer suggests a garden soil, perhaps predating the demolition of the old hall in the early nineteenth century, with the yellow clay found here and at the northern end of the trench being laid after that demolition.

The clay layers found within the trenches, particularly for Trench A and Trench C, points to the clay as representing a capping of the moat platform. This capping covered a possible garden soil and, from the finds in Trench A, seems to have taken place in the nineteenth century and to represent a raising of ground level on the moat platform following the demolition of the hall (Walker & Tindall, 1985, 44–46).

The small number of finds, mostly of a late date, were consistent with a large-scale removal of material from the site and suggested this had taken place in the early nineteenth century when the old hall was demolished and replaced by the farmhouse. The known or possible medieval finds appear to be all redeposited, being derived from

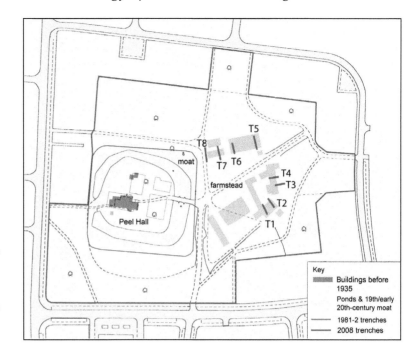

Plan of Peel Hall, Wythenshawe, showing the moated site, buildings and the location of the excavations.

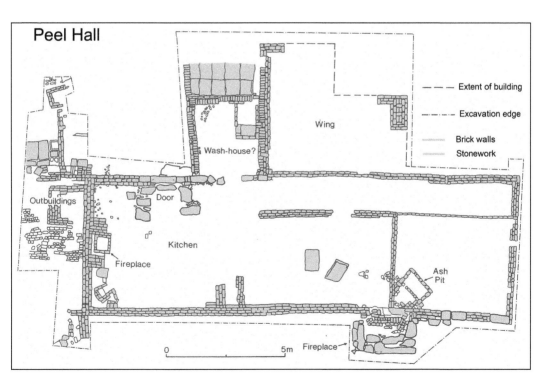

A plan of the excavated remains of the eighteenth and nineteenth-century farmhouse at Peel Hall uncovered in 1981. (Image courtesy of the Greater Manchester Archaeological Advisory Service)

contexts which also included eighteenth and nineteenth-century material. Physical evidence for the medieval hall building is limited to the fragments of grey-green ceramic roof tiles, which are likely to be of a mid to late medieval date and imply a building of some local status. The most detailed source of information on the early hall is provided by the probate inventory compiled in January 1665/6 after the death of Katherine Nicholls (Cheshire Records & Archives, wills). Twenty-six rooms are named in total. The inventory goes on to describe the hall and main ground-floor domestic rooms of the house, including the core and the main reception room of the building, the 'Great Parlour', the 'Little Closet on the side of the Parlour', and the 'Little Parlour'. The description suggests a general arrangement similar to that found in other halls of the period, including Wythenshawe.

A small community excavation was undertaken in February 2008 as part of the Dig Manchester project (Gregory, 2008, 3–21). Eight trenches to the east of the moat were dug with members of the South Manchester Archaeology Research Team and the South Trafford Archaeological Group. This work uncovered the remains of several outbuildings, including the remains of a barn and possible shippons/stables dating from the eighteenth and early nineteenth centuries. The remains included handmade brick walls and stone foundations and brick or stone cobbled yard surfaces.

The original dig of 1981 to 1982 highlighted the potential for survival of late medieval manor sites within the city, especially where these were located in parkland.

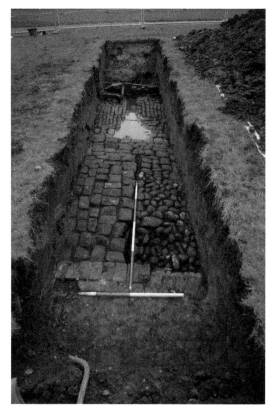

One of the 2008 trenches excavated over the site of the eighteenth and nineteenth-century farm building east of the Peel Hall moat as part of the Dig Manchester community archaeology project.

Dig 6

The First Mancunians – Manchester Runway 2 (1997 to 1998)

The construction of the second runway at Manchester Airport during the mid to late 1990s revealed evidence for the earliest settlers in Manchester: a series of Neolithic and Bronze Age farming communities. The survey and excavation work were undertaken by Gifford Archaeology, working with Manchester Airport PLC and the planning archaeologists for both Cheshire and Greater Manchester, since the new runway straddled the administrative boundary. Only those areas that needed to be excavated were investigated along the line of the new runway, which inevitably meant that some features extended beyond the excavation area (Nevell, 2008, 14–15).

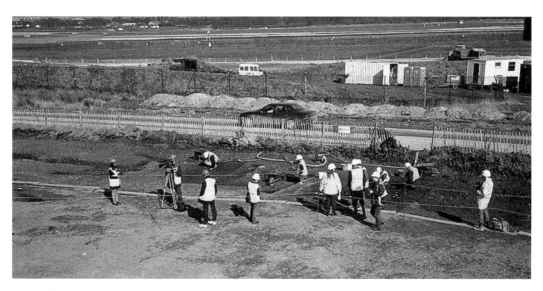

The Manchester Airport runway 2 excavations in 1997 revealed the earliest domestic occupation in the city, from the late Neolithic and early Bronze Age. (Image copyright GMAAS)

The remains of these earliest farming communities were discovered at Oversley Farm on the southern edge of the modern city, on the northern bank of the River Bollin. At roughly 73 metres above sea level, the site lies on the topographical boundary between the low-lying Cheshire plain to the south and west and the foothills of the Pennines to the north and east. It is by far the most important prehistoric site known within the boundaries of the twenty-first-century city and is one of the more important late prehistoric lowland sites within North West England.

The earliest activity, Phase 1, was represented by the remains of an Early Neolithic farming community, one of the first such communities to be established within North West England. These remains comprised a rectangular structure (Structure 1) around 7 metres by 10 metres formed by linear construction trenches and postholes, with a central hearth or cooking pit, dated to 3975–3675 calendar years BC (Garner, 2007, 12–14). This hearth contained fragments of pottery known as Grimston Ware, 267 sherds weighing 1.448 kg, but these may only have represented a small number of undecorated round-bottom bowls. The hearth also contained a high percentage of charcoal, fire-cracked stones and traces of barley and crop weed species, implying the cultivation of fields close by. Analysis of lipids within this pottery identified the presence of sheep or goat fat within the fabric of these bowls, suggesting they had been used for cooking (Garner, 2007, 20). A second hearth contained twenty-seven sherds (0.107 kg) of a granite-tempered pot.

The rectangular building was subsequently overlain by a second rectangular structure (Structure 2) with hearth deposits dated to 3015–2985 calendar years BC and containing

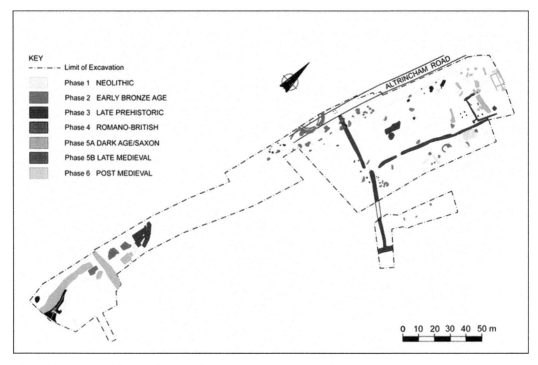

Plan of the excavated features beneath the second runway at Manchester Airport covering 5,000 years of occupation activity. (Image courtesy of the Greater Manchester Archaeological Advisory Service)

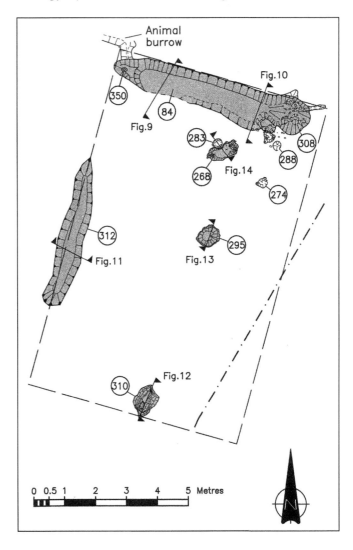

A plan of Manchester's first known house – a late Neolithic timber structure excavated at Manchester Airport. (Image courtesy of the Greater Manchester Archaeological Advisory Service)

a few sherds of pottery. A small number of granite-tempered pottery sherds were also associated with one of the second building's construction trenches. There were fifty-one Neolithic stone artefacts recovered from both structures, mostly from the hearth within Structure 1, and included fragments of flint knifes, blades, retouched flints and a pecked stone, as well as material from tool production (Garner, 2007, 21–24). Most of the flints were manufactured from dark grey/brown/black flint or chert that could have been recovered from the local glacial deposits.

The presence of two successive structures on virtually the same spot demonstrates either a continuity of occupation or a reoccupation and rebuilding on this site of sand and gravel above the River Bollin, suggesting that this land was regarded as favourable farming land in both periods. The gaps between these two phases raises the question of whether Oversley Farm was a permanent settlement or a seasonal base with religious or ritual significance, as has been suggested at other Neolithic domestic sites.

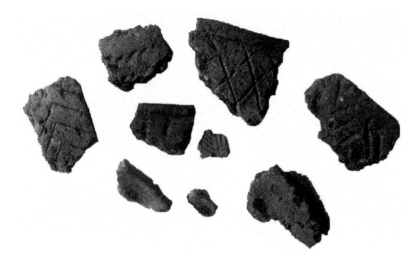

Some of the early Bronze Age pottery recovered from the round house at Manchester Airport. (Image courtesy of the Greater Manchester Archaeological Advisory Service)

Early Bronze Age activity on this site, Phase 2, was more extensive and was represented by four-post structures, a 'hollow way', buildings and pits across two sub-phases. These structures were associated with pit groups filled with midden deposits (some including pottery sherds) producing radio-carbon dates spanning the period 2135 to 1660 calendar years BC (Garner, 2007, 29–40).

The earliest Bronze Age activity comprised two structures, pits and the hollow way. Structure 3 lay on the north-eastern edge of the site and was an oval area defined by a construction trench enclosing a small area 6 metres by 4 metres and contained a pit 1.9 metres by 1.5 metres and 0.3 metres deep. Structure 4 was an oval-shaped post-built building, about 6.5 metres by 5.5 metres with a possible timber porch to the east, located about 40 m to the south of Structure 3. The interior included a hearth containing a fragment of a saddle quern-stone and a flat stone with a possible cup-mark, flint, and a sherd from a small pottery cup. The hollow way took the form of a linear depression around 7.5 metres wide and 0.5 metres deep running along the western edge of the excavation for around 300 metres.

The second phase of Early Bronze Age activity took the form of several new structures, forming a small open farming settlement, and probably represented the high point of prehistoric activity on the site. This activity was centred around the middle of the hollow way and a large round building. Structure 5, of which only half lay within the excavation area, was defined by a circular trench, 12.5 metres wide, with an entrance to the east. To the north of this was a small four-post square timber granary building, 1.4 metres by 1.4 metres (Structure 6), a second possible square timber granary building about 2 metres south of the round house Structure 5, and a rectangular post structure, 5 metres by 6 metres, located within the hollow way north-east of Structure 6. During this period the hollow way was partially infilled with midden deposits (representing sixty-three different collared urns) (Garner, 2007, 41–49).

A third phase of Early Bronze Age activity saw the hollow way surfaced in rough metalling for the first time, with pits and burnt deposits and domestic waste, but no structures, focussed along its length.

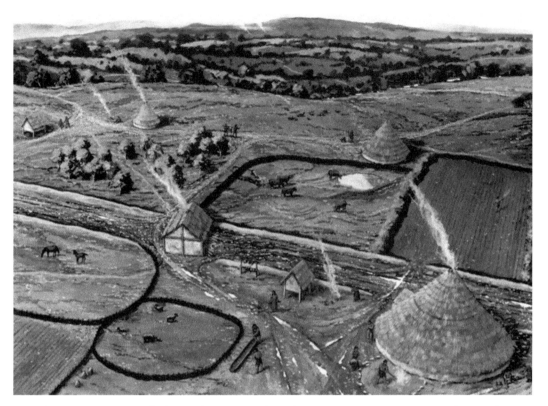

A reconstruction of the early Bronze Age farming community at Manchester Airport. (Image courtesy of the Greater Manchester Archaeological Advisory Service)

Up to 2,000 sherds of Early Bronze Age pottery were recovered from these phases, including beakers, cordoned and collared urns, incense/pygmy cups, and food vessels. Around 315 sherds, weighing 1.57 kg, came from the first burst of Early Bronze Age occupation. The rest of the pottery came from two later periods of Early Bronze Activity, which produced pottery sherds weighing 6.8 kg, nearly 60 per cent of all the pottery recovered from this period, and a smaller number of sherds from the third period of activity, weighing 0.88 kg. A large quantity of Early Bronze Age lithic artefacts, including scrapers and a barbed and tanged arrowhead, were also recovered (Garner, 2007, 87–97).

Oversley Farm appears to have continued in, perhaps sporadic, use as an agricultural settlement throughout the first millennium BC. This was shown by a few dozen sherds of Later Bronze Age pottery associated with a scatter of pits, a possible Iron Age four-post timber structure, and three sherds of possible Iron Age pottery. Roman activity took the form of the reuse of the hollow way as a road, a scatter of pits and an oval post structure (Structure 11) 9 metres by 7 metres, all associated with pottery of the late first to third centuries, a shale armlet, lead weight and copper-alloy brooch (Garner, 2007, 102–119). The small number of features and the ephemeral structural evidence for the later prehistoric and Roman periods suggests less intensive occupation, with the focus of any settlement activity having moved elsewhere.

Dig 7

Hanging Ditch and Bridge, Medieval Manchester (1998–2002)

After the completion in 1989 of the Roman fort excavations on the corner of Beaufort Street and Duke Street in Castlefield, there was a lull in the investigation of the archaeology of the city centre. The confirmation of the place of developer-funded archaeology in the planning process, with the issuing of Planning Policy Guidance Note Number 16 in November 1990, led to the steady growth of professional archaeology in England throughout the 1990s. An increasing amount of archaeological work was undertaken across the Manchester city region ahead of redevelopment work such as the building of the second runway at Manchester airport (Nevell, 2019a, 111). However, there was little excavation work within the city centre itself during this period.

That changed after an IRA bomb damaged much of the historic late medieval and post-medieval core of Manchester city centre on 15 June 1996 (Nevell, 2008, 9). The City Council's subsequent blueprint for the renewal of the city centre around the cathedral, Cheetham's School of Music, Hanging Ditch, the Shambles, and St Ann's Square, became an opportunity to excavate the remains of the later medieval industrial city. The Greater Manchester Archaeological Unit (under the leadership of County Archaeologist Robina McNeil and her deputy Norman Redhead) took the lead in providing archaeology planning advice for the biggest rebuilding project within Manchester since the Victorian period. The archaeological work ahead of the first part of the reconstruction work around the cathedral in 1998 and 1999 threw new light on Manchester's late medieval defences and industries, including the discovery and recording of the well-preserved remains of a local leather industry and the city's oldest bridge, from the fourteenth century.

The most mysterious of these remains was the line of Hanging Ditch, a ditch-like feature that surrounded the cathedral and Cheetham's until it was filled in at the end of the seventeenth century. It can still be traced as a curving road alignment along the road of the same name, Corporation Street and Todd Street. In the late eighteenth century, the local antiquarian John Whitaker suggested that this curving line represented an early defensive ditch, cutting off the spur between the River Irwell and the River Irk. Whitaker

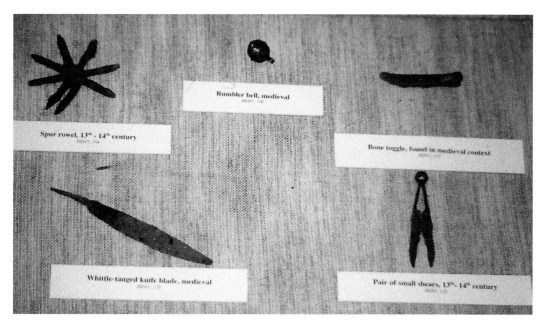

Medieval leatherwork and metalwork recovered from Hanging Ditch in central Manchester during the excavations in 1998.

himself believed the ditch to be Roman in origin, whilst Roeder proposed an Iron Age date (Roeder, 1899). Excavation work in 1998 and 1999 (Nevell, 2008) confirmed the line of this ditch and showed that it was a large feature roughly 10 metres wide and more than 5 metres deep in places. Topographically, its origin suggests that it was originally a meltwater channel from the end of the last ice age, but no finds earlier than the later medieval period have so far been uncovered, suggesting two possible contexts for the deepening and extension of Hanging Ditch (Morris, 1983, 47). The first of these is that Hanging Ditch was dug for the late Anglo-Saxon fortified settlement mentioned in the *Anglo-Saxon Chronicle* (Morris, 1983, 15). The second suggested origin is that it was dug to surround the later medieval town. At the moment the weight of the archaeological evidence favours this latter, more prosaic, explanation.

The most extensive investigations of Hanging Ditch were the excavations undertaken by the University of Manchester in 1998 and 1999 in the area known as the Cathedral Gates between Cateaton Street and the cathedral, a site around 50 metres east of Hanging Bridge. This work was undertaken prior to the erection on this site of the Wellington Inn and Sinclair's public house, dismantled and removed from the Old Shambles a few hundred meters to the south. The northern part of the excavation site had once formed part of the post-medieval churchyard of the parish church, later the cathedral, and included more than 200 burials. The southern part of the site was crossed from east to west by the line of Hanging Ditch, which lay below about 3 metres of cellarage and was revealed in section. The excavation showed that the waterborne deposits within the natural post-glacial channel had been cut to form a broad ditch (Nevell, 2008, 43–46). The date at which the cut was made is not at present known,

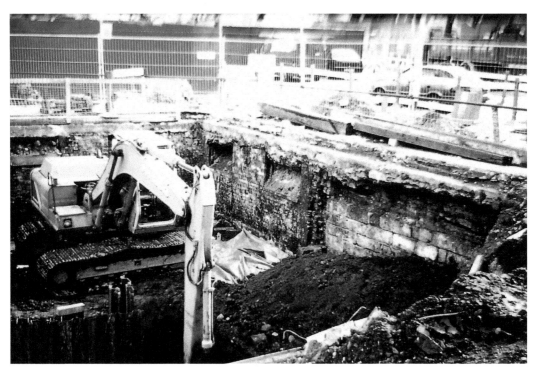

The excavation of the medieval boundary feature known as Hanging Ditch, surrounding the parish church and Cheetham's School, revealed that it had been backfilled during the early post-medieval period and property boundaries built over its course.

but the fill of this ditch contained artefacts and material dating from the fourteenth and fifteenth centuries. These finds included pottery, bone, wood, metal and more than 200 pieces of leather work (both offcuts and leather artefacts such as shoes and a sword scabbard) and amounts to by far the largest assemblage of medieval material from Manchester (Walker, 2000, 5). From the excavation it is clear that Hanging Ditch was being infilled by rubbish during the later medieval period, to the extent that by the close of the sixteenth century the line of the ditch was being reclaimed for building purposes.

Spanning the western end of Hanging Ditch is the third oldest surviving structure within the city centre (after the eastern Roman fort gateway and Manchester Cathedral): Hanging Bridge. The earliest known mention of Hanging Bridge occurs in 1343, when it is documented as 'Hengand Bridge' in a property deed (Morris, 1983, 48). No documentary evidence has been found either for when the bridge was first constructed or for the date of any alterations to its fabric. However, a link has often been made with the major building works in the town during the early fifteenth century, such as the rebuilding of the parish church as a much grander edifice served by a college of priests and the construction of a new residence to house that college. The primary function of the bridge can be interpreted as providing an approach to the church from the south, in particular from Deansgate (itself a medieval street) and the town's medieval marketplace (situated in the angle between Deansgate and Cateaton Street).

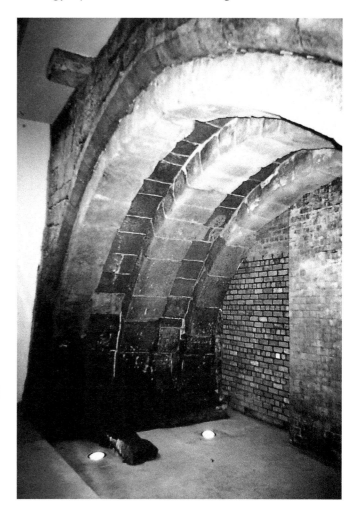

Hanging Bridge, now part of the cathedral visitor centre, dates from the fourteenth century and gave access to the late medieval parish church. It is the oldest surviving bridge within the city.

Survey work at Hanging Bridge between 2000 and 2002, during ground and building works undertaken for the conversion of adjacent properties into the cathedral visitor centre, revealed further details of this intriguing structure. Most of the known bridge fabric is of a single phase of construction, with the only indication of date being in the use of the four-centred Perpendicular arch, which has suggested a date of between around 1350 and 1500 (Morris, 1983, 48). The northern end of the western face includes a section of more irregular stonework, which has been suggested as being part of an earlier bridge, perhaps with a timber superstructure (Morris, 1983, 48; Nevell, 2008, 44–45). It is possible that this earlier bridge included the lower steps at the base of the south side of the southern arch, which appear to be relatively crude in form. The underside of the arch above these stepped foundations may include a reused chamfered block. Again, no firmer evidence has been found for the date of such an earlier bridge to compliment and refine the documentary evidence for Hanging Bridge being in existence by 1343.

Dig 8

Medieval Iron Making – Whitecarr Lane, Wythenshawe (2003)

By the beginning of the twenty-first century developer-funded archaeological work was firmly embedded within the planning process of the Manchester city region. This meant many areas that had never seen any archaeological research were being investigated for the first time. These were usually small, discrete, urban pieces of land, but as the discoveries ahead of the building of the second runway at Manchester Airport had shown, the rural fringes of the city had great potential for new discoveries. One such rural fringe was the green corridor straddling the southern border between the Borough of Trafford and the City of Manchester along the line of Fairywell Brook. The building of a water pipeline by United Utilities between the Hale Waste Water Treatment Works and Wythenshawe provided a rare opportunity to look at a transect through this rural fringe.

United Utilities facilitated the investigation of an area 10 metres by 15 metres immediately west of the pipeline easement, around 20 metres north of the point where the water pipeline easement crossed Whitecarr Lane in Hale Barns. The work was undertaken between May and July 2003 by the University of Manchester Archaeological Unit, who investigated the unexpected remains for Bronze Age activity and late medieval iron smelting first discovered during watching brief work ahead of the pipeline construction. These discoveries included a roasting hearth and fragments of a late medieval bloomery iron furnace (Nevell, 2008, 47).

The prehistoric activity was sketchy, but nevertheless noteworthy. A straight ditch (Feature 117), running north to south, with a terminus at its southern end, was excavated along the eastern edge of the easement and traced for around 5 metres. This contained two Late Neolithic/Early Bronze Age lithic scrapers. This suggests some form of land division in this area during the late third or early second millennium BC, echoing the prehistoric finds at Oversley Farm, 5 km to the south.

The rest of the evidence excavated was for the primary smelting of iron ore. In terms of the form of the bloomery itself, all the examples from Greater Manchester followed a similar pattern with a bloomery smelting shaft furnace in the form of a free-standing cylindrical structure built from clay (often locally sourced) formed around a wooden armature such as willow withies. At Whitecarr Lane the furnace lay in the north-eastern

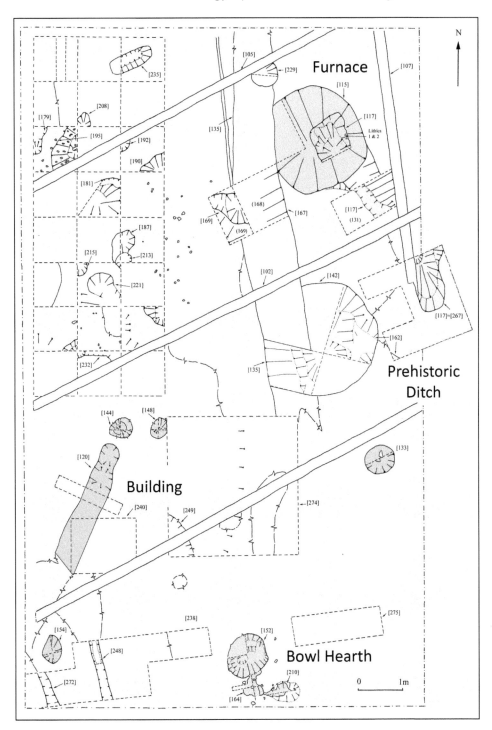

Plan of the late medieval ironworking site excavated in 2003 at Whitecarr Lane on the Hale Barns/Wythenshawe border in southern Manchester. This was the first medieval ironworking site located within the city boundaries.

corner of the site. Just the very bottom of the furnace survived (Pit 115), which was about 2.4 metres in diameter and 0.23 metres deep. Once the smelting process was over, the bloom had to be further worked in order to remove any slag and impurities that remained within its matrix. This operation was normally undertaken, whilst the bloom was still hot from the furnace, in a bowl hearth. South of the furnace was an oval-shaped feature (Pit 152), 1.02 metres in diameter and 0.27 metres deep, which appears to have been just such a feature. A scatter of seven postholes at the southern end of the site may have been the remains of a temporary open-sided rectangular shed, roughly 4 metres by 5 metres, for the iron workers.

A total of 50.62 kg (approximately 990 fragments) of industrial waste from Whitecarr Lane was recovered. Most of this assemblage (25.25 kg, 657 pieces) consisted of heavily broken fragments of non-diagnostic slag with a highly vesicular structure. The next largest proportion of the assemblage was composed of tap slag (18.60 kg, 247 fragments). The presence of at least one plano-convex smithing hearth bottom (Pit 115) shows that iron smithing in bowl hearths was being undertaken. The remainder of the material is likely to derive from smelting. Most of this material (39.05 kg, 624 fragments) came from contexts within this single pit, although some slag was recovered from the pit to the south of the furnace (Askew et al., 2009).

The industrial waste from Whitecarr Lane is typical of the products of the bloomery furnace commonly in use for the smelting of iron in Britain from the Iron Age to the sixteenth century but still used in some areas into the eighteenth century (Day & Tylecote, 1991). Fragments of slag fused to green glazed pottery suggest a *terminus post*

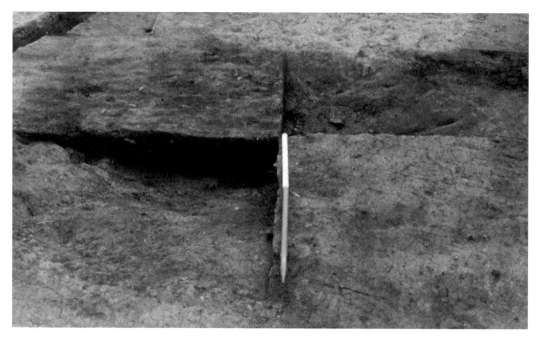

The late medieval iron furnace during excavations at Whitecarr Lane by the University of Manchester Archaeological Unit.

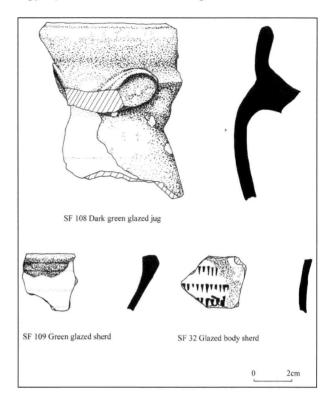

SF 108 Dark green glazed jug

SF 109 Green glazed sherd   SF 32 Glazed body sherd

0   2cm

Some of the late medieval pottery found associated with the iron furnace at Whitecarr Lane.

quem for the furnace's operation in the fourteenth to fifteenth centuries. At this date the use of a water-powered bloomery is likely, though the only evidence to support this is the adjacent course of the Fairywell Brook.

Lowland evidence for medieval bloomery furnaces in the North West is very rare; the majority of examples known are from the uplands of the region (Brennand with Chitty & Nevell, 2006, 132–3).They are known from 200 examples from Cumbria and several from the Rossendale uplands (Morris, 1983). Within Greater Manchester there are eight identified and investigated sites, with the best-known sites in the uplands around Castleshaw, dating to the twelfth to fourteenth centuries (Redhead, 1995 & 2004), and Holcombe Moor, dating to the twelfth and thirteenth centuries. However, there is growing evidence for lowland bloomeries in several parts of Greater Manchester, with fourteenth to fifteenth-century examples recently excavated at Cut Acre and Gadbury Fold, both in Wigan (Gregory, 2019), and now at Whitecarr Lane in Hale Barns, Trafford. Archaeologically, the origin of the iron ore used at Whitecarr Lane is difficult to pinpoint but in the lowlands of Greater Manchester the chief source was probably bog iron.

The evidence for bloomer smelting at Whitecarr Lane is an important addition to the lowland evidence for North West England as a whole. At the very least this fragmentary activity demonstrates that the late medieval economy of Manchester was more than just crop growing and hunting, and during the sixteenth and seventeenth centuries another industry would begin its long rise to dominance in the city: textiles.

Dig 9

Living in the Industrial City – Hardman Street (2002 and 2004)

A small area of the city at the top of Deansgate provided the first detailed look at life in the Georgian boom town of Manchester in 2002 and 2004. Workers' housing had been excavated before in the city, at White Lion Street in 1972 and at Marsden Court in 1982. However, the excavation between Hardman Street and Atkinson Street, immediately north of the John Rylands Library, was the first dig to specifically target the workers' housing and urban forms of the industrial city of the eighteenth and nineteenth centuries through the planning process. It also produced the most significant assemblage of finds from the industrial city since the excavation of Marsden Court in the early 1980s.

After some initial research in 2002 excavation work was undertaken by the University of Manchester Archaeology Unit in April and May 2004 that identified cellar dwellings hemmed in by an upstanding textile mill, soda water works and an eighteenth-century felt hat works run by the Bower family (Nevell, 2008).

Six main phases of construction were uncovered (Gregory 2005). Phase 1 was dated to the early to mid-eighteenth century and saw the construction of a pair of three-storey buildings, 11 metres wide and probably no more than 5 metres deep, fronting the former Cupid's Alley prior to 1734 (now known as Hardman Street). Only the rear rooms were available for excavation. These were the remains of workshop dwellings, a type of proto-industrial building used for the hand manufacture of textiles, shoes, or hats, and still to be found in some numbers in the Northern Quarter area of the city. A square building, which appears to have functioned as a dyeing house, was constructed around the same time in the yard to the north of one western workshop dwelling, suggesting that hat manufacturing began on the site during the early to mid-eighteenth century. The square brick-built single-storey structure contained a circular furnace, 2.4 metres in diameter and 0.98 metres high with a central flue, on which would have stood a vat for the dyeing liquid. There was a small square brick chimney to the rear of the furnace.

Phase 2 dated to the mid-eighteenth century and saw the remodelling and expansion of the hat works building. The square building was extended to the east and a second brick-built furnace, around 1.6 metres in diameter and 0.5 metres high, erected in

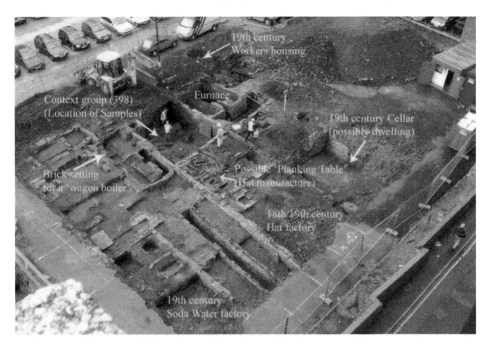

The Hardman Street excavations, off Deansgate in the city centre, were the first extensive investigation of the eighteenth and nineteenth-century industrial city. The site encompassed a felt hat works, soda works and workers' housing.

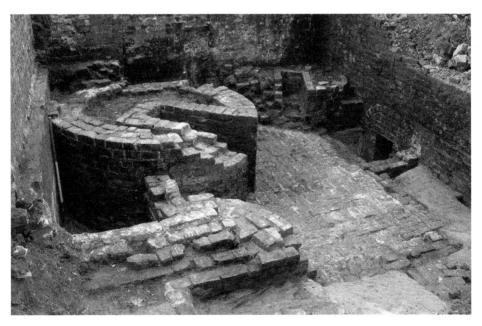

The mid to late eighteenth-century dye vat bases and furnaces at Hardman Street. This was part of the felt hat works run by the Bower family, one of the leading merchant families in Manchester at the time.

the north-eastern corner of the room. Phase 3, dated to the mid to late eighteenth century, saw the addition of a second brick building to the south of the dye room, effectively creating a single structure. This new room had a brick floor, sunk into which were a series of four ash pits and four brick-lined soak-away channels, and a brick setting. These features suggested that the building had been sued as a 'planking room', where the rabbit fur was soaked in sulphuric acid and squeezed to create the felt mat that formed the body of a hat. After drying and shaping, this would be dyed in the adjacent room.

These remains were associated with the Bower family, whose house lay immediately to the north in the early eighteenth century. Miles Bower Sr and Miles Bower Jr were prominent figures in eighteenth-century Manchester and derived their wealth from felt hat manufacture, the city becoming a major centre for this type of production during this period. Miles Bower Sr seems to have continued to live at the house on Deansgate until his death in 1780, at the age of eighty-five. According to one tradition it was Miles Bower Sr who laid the foundation stone of the Manchester Infirmary in Piccadilly in 1755 (Axon, 1886, 91; Nevell with Grimsditch & Hradil, 2007, 7–9).

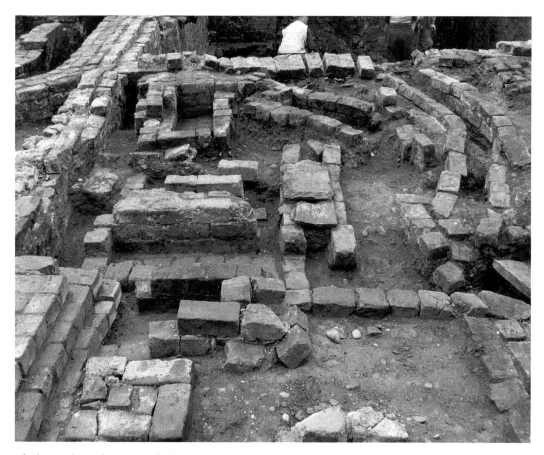

The late eighteenth-century planking shop, where the felt hat bodies were made, at Hardman Street.

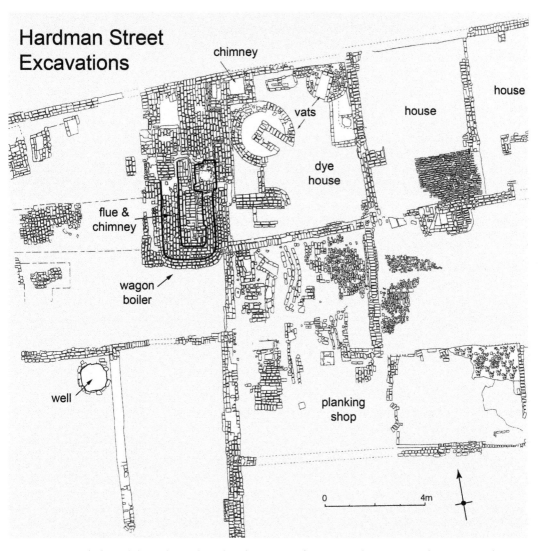

Hardman Street Excavations

chimney

vats

house

house

dye house

flue & chimney

wagon boiler

well

planking shop

0   4m

Excavated plan of the eighteenth and early nineteenth-century phases at Hardman Street showing the remains of the soda works (well and wagon boiler), hat works (planking shop and dye vats) and the basements of workers' housing.

During Phase 4, dating to the late eighteenth century, further additions and modifications were made to the hat works, whilst a chemical soda works was established in the adjacent premises to the east. This soda works was probably built by Samuel Thompstone in 1801. The artefactual and documentary evidence suggests that the works was subsequently taken over by J. H. Cuff in the late nineteenth century. Significantly, the potential establishment of the soda works in 1801 would make it an early example, particularly as large-scale soda water manufacturing did not begin until 1792 with the establishment of Schweppes's soda water factory in Drury Lane, London.

The surviving archaeological remains took the form of a well, 1.1 metres in diameter, and the base of a wagon boiler, 5.2 metres by 3.2 metres, both important elements in the manufacturing process. Further features, which probably relate to those processes requiring a heat source, included three ash pits discovered to the west of the wagon boiler, whilst the numerous finds of pipettes, burettes and glass storage vessels, or 'carbouys', from within the works were certainly associated with some form of chemical manufacturing. By the early nineteenth century it appears that the chemical works was engaged in soda water and ginger beer manufacturing, following Schweppes's introduction of this type of beverage into Britain in the 1820s. Archaeologically the production of these beverages is perhaps evidenced through structures that would have supported a gas holder and an associated soda water engine, which was in itself potentially powered by the wagon boiler. Another structure, which probably related to this phase of use, was a small forge that might have been used to produce metal bottle fittings needed to secure a cork or stopper.

Phases 5 and 6 dated to the early nineteenth and late nineteenth to early twentieth centuries respectively. The workshop dwellings were spilt into separate tenements and the cellars used as domestic accommodation during Phase 5.

Most of the artefacts recovered from the site belonged to the nineteenth-century phases and two middens associated with the soda works and found at the rear (northern) end of this part of the site. They included 162 kg of glass in 971 fragments, many of which were fragments of press-moulded torpedo or bomb-shaped glass bottles associated with the soda works. There were also standard beer and pontil-shaped bottles from deposits associated with the workshop dwellings. There were 2,095 sherds of pottery found across the site, with a notable grouping from the backfill of the dye room (175 sherds), dominated by stoneware types (roughly half of all the pottery) from the nineteenth century. Some of these had maker's names embossed on them, the most frequent of which was for 'John Keal & Sons, Wine and Spirit Merchants, Manchester'. There was a smaller grouping of finewares, typical of late eighteenth and early nineteenth-century kitchen and tableware forms. Only a few sherds were identified from seventeenth and eighteenth-century fabrics.

The hat works and soda works remained in use until the late nineteenth century, whilst the former workshop dwellings remained in use into the early twentieth century. All these properties were demolished in the mid-twentieth century.

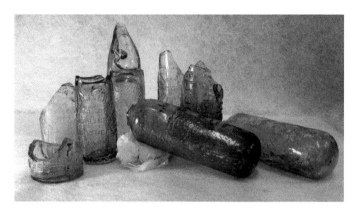

Some of the glass bottles recovered from the early nineteenth-century soda works uncovered at Hardman Street.

Dig 10

Bottling the Past – The Jersey Street Glassworks (2003)

Manchester once had an extensive glass industry, which flourished from the late eighteenth century to the early twentieth century, encouraged by the availability of cheap coal, cheap labour and an extensive transport network. The Jersey Street works in Ancoats was one of the largest of the city's glassworks. In 2003 redevelopment represented the first opportunity to investigate archaeologically this particular branch of Manchester's secondary industries. The excavation work was undertaken by Oxford Archaeology North and revealed the remains of three glass furnaces of the nineteenth century (Nevell, 2008, 131–133).

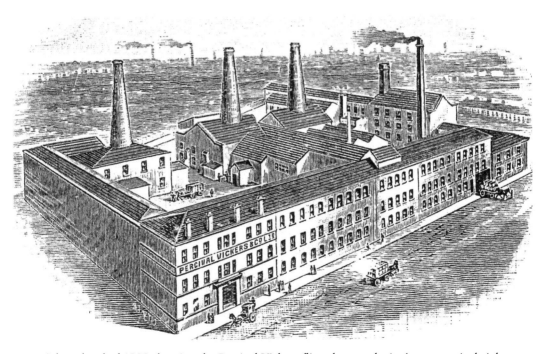

A letterhead of 1902 showing the Percival Vickers flint glass works in Ancoats at its height.

The first glassworks within the Manchester region was recorded in 1795, whilst the last site, the Perserverance Glassworks of Fredrick Hampson in Duncan Street, Salford, closed as late as 1964. At least twenty-five flint glass works have been identified, operated by thirty-nine different business partnerships, in Manchester and Salford during this period. The industry in the city was notable for its rapid expansion, in part resulting from the lifting of the excise tax on glassware in 1845, and equally rapid decline in the early twentieth century due to the unregulated competition from overseas. By 1833 there were already six firms listed in the local trade directory for the city. However, the prosperity of the Manchester industry was based upon the introduction of the glass press during the 1850s, led by Percival Vickers & Company.

Historically, the Percival Vickers site was the largest glassworks in the city and was in operation during the years between 1844 and 1914. The history of this site has been studied by Manchester Region Industrial Archaeology Society and the surviving office and warehouse structures studied with the University of Manchester. Percival Yates & Vickers's flint glass works at 64 Jersey Street was established in 1844. By 1863, the Jersey Street works had 373 employees, including forty-three boys less than thirteen years of age. By 1869, the maps suggest that two kilns were in operation, increased to three by 1880, marking the peak of the company's fortunes (Bone, 2005). The warehouse/office building range is the only part of the complex surviving above ground. It is a three-phased, brick structure with three storeys and a roof of king-post trusses, braced by bolts, renovated in the late 1990s. Internally, it has wooden floors supported by cast iron columns and there was a cellar at the northern end of the range with a fireproof brick barrel-vaulted ceiling. The original 1844 building is probably represented by the southern ten bays of the structure, with the two subsequent phases adding initially nine and then eight more bays by 1880. There are various blocked doorways and windows at the southern end of the south-eastern elevation that may be connected with a number of the excavated structures to the rear (Champness & Nevell, 2003).

The excavations in 2003 uncovered three pot-type furnaces and an annealing house and, most importantly, recorded variations in the design of the glass furnaces that demonstrated technological developments in the later nineteenth century previously unknown during this period. The two primary kilns, built in the 1840s, were 6.4 metres in diameter with furnace walls 0.5 metres thick surviving to a depth of 2 metres and were each capable of holding ten pots. The core of each furnace was at foundation level 2.7 metres thick and each was encircled by a narrow brick-lined and flagstone-capped channel. The adjoining annealing house, where the blown vessels were transferred to an oven for controlled cooling, was also from this initial period. The third, most easterly, furnace was added in the 1870s and was more advanced technically. It was 7.16 metres in diameter, with exterior walls 0.84 metres thick and a furnace diameter of 4.6 metres and was capable of holding ten pots (Miller, 2007, 19–24).

Located between the original two furnaces (Furnaces 1 and 2) was an annealing house. Annealing was a critical part of the glass-making process, allowing the glass vessels to cool at a set rate. Without this process different parts of vessels would cool at different rates, setting up stresses that could crack or shatter the glass. The

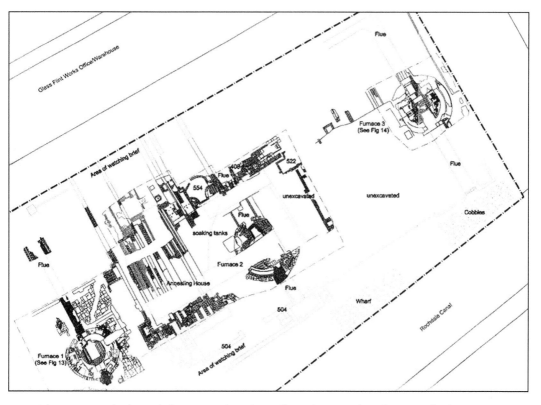

The excavated plan of the Percival Vickers flint glass works, showing the location of the three nineteenth-century glass kilns and the annealing house. (Image courtesy of Oxford Archaeology North)

foundations of the brick-built annealing house were extensive and took the form of six brick-lined channels, each 0.65 metres wide and 16.4 metres long, aligned north to south, and arranged in two groups of three. The brick and flagged floors were all blackened by exposure to temperatures of 500 to 600 degrees Celsius. The annealing furnace probably had its own heat source, rather than reusing the spent gases from the neighbouring furnaces, though this source was not located. Each channel had incised grooves running off centre along its length for guiding the wheeled carriers loaded with the newly blown glass products (Miller, 2007, 23–4). The glass products would have spent many hours in the annealing house, allowing them to cool at a steady rate.

All three kilns excavated at the Percival Vickers site were reverberatory furnaces worked at temperatures between 1,400 and 1,600 degrees Celsius, which was needed to melt the raw materials and ensure any gaseous bubbles formed during the melting process were eliminated. The air for combustion was drawn through two flues, a feature common to many other Manchester glassworks but not often found elsewhere. Regulating the volume of air passing through the intake flue was an important part of the manufacturing process. It was done by placing a shutter across the flue that would

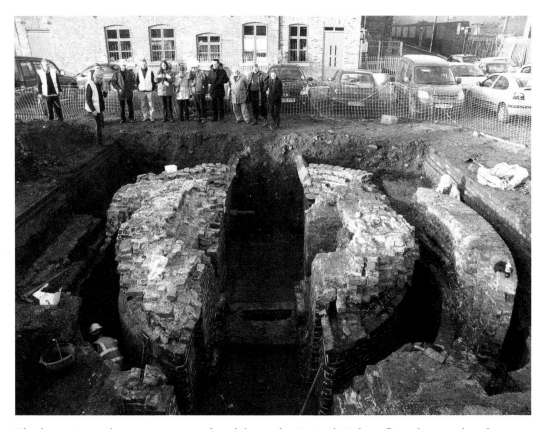

The late nineteenth-century eastern glass kiln at the Percival Vickers flint glass works after excavation by Oxford Archaeology North in 2003. This contained a number of innovative features known only from these archaeological excavations. (Image courtesy of the Greater Manchester Archaeological Advisory Service)

have been operated from the furnace floor. The third furnace shows evidence for the introduction of ceramic pipes in the siege area that would have allowed the combustion air to be preheated whilst the introduction of a Frisbie feeder allowed a deeper and more consistently packed coal bed, so improving firing. Both innovations would have improved the thermal efficiency of the kiln.

The innovative features identified during the excavation of the furnaces are unique in this period. Their presence may explain why Percival Vickers was able to continue in production using pot-type furnaces at a time when the more fuel-efficient and thermal-efficient Siemens-designed gas-fired furnace, which used a recycled heat system, became commonplace in the 1880s in the major glass-making centres of Birmingham and St Helens (Miller, 2007, 27–8).

Dig 11

I Dig Moston Hall (2003–5)

The early twenty-first century saw a revival of community-focussed archaeological work in the city, led by the 'I Dig Moston' project. Moston is a suburb on the northern side of Manchester overlooking the Medlock Valley and Broadhurst Clough. Led by one of the local councillors, Paul Murphy, a local community group set out to explore the area's origins and along the way help to improve local community cohesion and identity.

This north Manchester local community approached and were helped by the staff of the Greater Manchester Archaeological Unit and the University of Manchester Archaeology Unit in uncovering the late medieval and post-medieval manor house, the community archaeologist, Simon Askew, providing the professional focus for the team. The project set a pattern for future voluntary and professional partnerships in community digs within the city region (Nevell, 2013, 68–69; Murphy, 2015, 89–90).

The site of Moston Hall in Broadhurst Park was excavated between 2003 and 2005. This was only the second late medieval hall site to be investigated within the city boundaries, the first being Peel Hall in Wythenshawe. The history of Moston Hall begins with the de Moston family, who owned the estate in the thirteenth and fourteenth centuries. The first known member of this family was Richard de Moston, who is documented in 1276. The de Mostons paid a freehold rent for their estate to

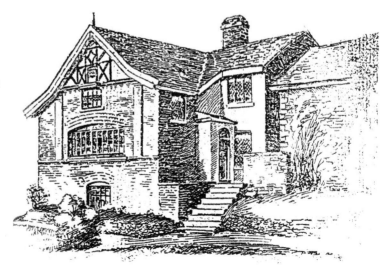

A drawing of Moston Hall from 1820. Moston Hall was the focus of the 'I Dig Moston' community archaeology project and later part of the 'Dig Manchester' project. (Image courtesy of the Greater Manchester Archaeological Advisory Service)

another local family, the Nuthursts. In about 1400 ownership of Moston Hall passed from the de Mostons to the Radcliffes, one of the oldest and most prominent families in Lancashire and resident at Ordsall Hall in Salford. The manor passed through the Radcliffe line until the mid-sixteenth century. In 1541 a document, which makes the first direct mention of Moston Hall, states that the Shacklock family, minor gentry, occupied it as tenants. The death of Edward Shacklock in 1663 led to the sale of the hall to Edward Cheetham. The earlier timber hall was leased to tenants, in the eighteenth century was rebuilt in brick and in the mid-nineteenth century was owned and lived in by T. W. Leigh Hilton, a local landowner who clad the front of the hall in fashionable mock-timber framing. The hall and estate were gifted to the city in 1919 and Broadhurst Park was laid out in the 1920s. After a period of neglect the hall was demolished in 1961 (Garratt, 2009, 6–9).

The archaeological investigations stripped an area of about 46 metres by about 52 metres over three seasons, revealing the courtyard hall complex, including the late medieval timber-framed hall and a stone and timber farmyard range of the eighteenth and nineteenth centuries. The earliest activity on the site was a prehistoric ditch running east to west, underneath the remains of the barn and outbuildings. The feature was substantial, measuring 4 metres wide and 1.5 metres deep and extending 20 metres across the site. This ditch probably cut off the 'landward' side of the promontory of land formed by Dean Clough. Two artefacts were found in association with the ditch where it lay under the stone foundations of the large rectangular barn. These were flint tools used during

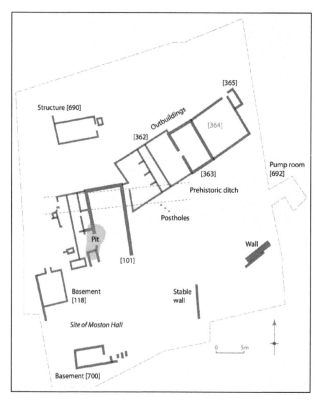

A plan of the excavated hall and farm buildings at Moston Hall, as excavated by the University of Manchester Archaeological Unit from 2003 to 2005. Also shown is the location of the prehistoric ditch and the late medieval rubbish pit beneath the hall complex. (Image courtesy of the Greater Manchester Archaeological Advisory Service)

the Bronze Age for shaping wood and scraping fat from the inside of animal hides. The presence of the ditch suggests that some form of small settlement may have existed on this promontory between the River Medlock and Dean Clough during this period.

Although remains of the late medieval Moston Hall did not survive, probably removed by the building of the post-medieval brick hall, pottery from the thirteenth to fifteenth centuries were recovered from across the site. An oval pit beneath the barn, 8 metres by 4 metres and 0.5 metres deep, contained a charcoal layer from burning. This was radiocarbon dated to the period 1173 to 1400. Probably in use as a rubbish pit, this feature contained fifteenth and sixteenth-century pottery, a cattle jaw and a piece of stitched leather, probably used as an axe sheath (Garratt, 2009, 26–27).

The earliest buildings to survive on the site were the barn. The barn had sandstone foundations and was 14 metres by 7 metres in plan with eastern and western-facing opposed doorways, indicating a use for threshing grain crops. Based on their typology, the character of the stone foundations and pottery found in a pit below the barn, it is probable that the barn was constructed during the sixteenth century. A stone porch was added to the western entrance, whilst other alterations in brick during the nineteenth century included internal divisions and soakaways and extensions to the north-west, probably to covert the barn into a cowshed or shippon. The barn was demolished during the 1930s. To the north-east of the barn was a small outbuilding of similar sixteenth-century date, 5 metres by 8 metres, also with stone foundations (Garratt, 2019, 22–29).

East of the stone barn were the remains of a further range of brick-built outbuildings built during the late eighteenth or early nineteenth centuries and aligned west to east. A second brick-built structure was added, abutting to the east, in the mid-nineteenth century. The excavated plan shows a series of entrances and internal partitions, whilst photographic evidence shows a range of two-storey barns with a hayloft above. These structures were in use as shippons (Garratt, 2019, 30–31).

Finally, the fragmentary remains of the post-medieval hall were located to the south of the two barn ranges. These deposits had been badly damaged during the demolition of the hall and subsequent landscaping in 1961. What survived were the remains of two brick-built basements. To the rear, or north, of the building was a small cellared wing, 4 metres by 6 metres, added between 1848 and 1891, with a brick-built cellar with lime-washed walls, probably used for cold storage. The front of the hall was marked by

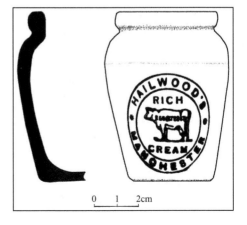

A drawing of a creamery jar found at Moston Hall. Cow shippons dominated the agricultural buildings at the hall site in the nineteenth and early twentieth centuries. Hailwood, named on the jar, was a local dairy firm. (Image courtesy of the Greater Manchester Archaeological Advisory Service)

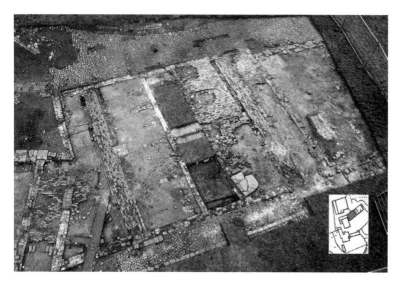

An aerial view of the nineteenth and early twentieth-century cow barns during excavation at Moston Hall. (Image courtesy of the Greater Manchester Archaeological Advisory Service)

a brick and stone-built half-cellar, 7 metres wide by 3 metres and surviving up to 1 metre deep. Steps gave access to the basement from the floor above. This probably marked the gabled front of the building seen on contemporary drawings and photographs and dated from the early nineteenth-century rebuild.

The 'I Dig Moston' project enabled the direct involvement in the excavation of local residents and disadvantaged groups, engaged around 1,000 local school children from across the city in the project and was visited by over 3,000 people during a series of open days. As one resident commented, the dig was 'the most talked-about happening in Moston for years.' Furthermore, it led directly to the Dig Manchester project, a city-wide community archaeology scheme supported by the Heritage Lottery Fund that ran from 2004 to 2008 (Garratt, 2009, 14; Nevell, 2014, 35).

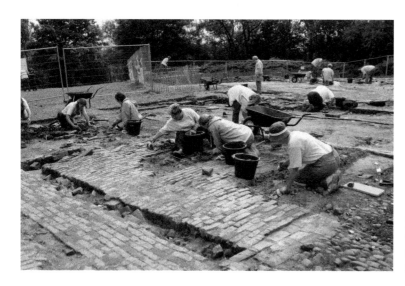

Dig Manchester volunteers working on the Moston Hall site in 2005.

Dig Manchester – Northenden Corn Mill (2005–2006)

The substantial remains of a water-powered corn mill at Northenden, on the southern bank of the River Mersey, were excavated in 2005 and 2006. This is the only corn mill to have been excavated within the city. It was investigated as part of the Dig Manchester project, a city-wide community archaeology scheme supported by the Heritage Lottery

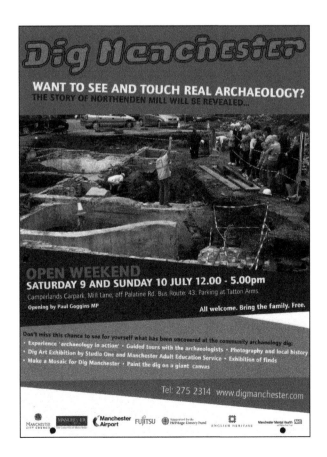

A poster for the Northenden Mill dig open day, run as part of the Dig Manchester community archaeology project.

Fund, overseen by Robina McNeal, the county archaeologist, that ran from 2004 to 2008 (Nevell, 2013; Nevell, 2019). A successor to 'I Dig Moston' (see Dig 11) and led by community archaeologist Simon Askew from the University of Manchester Archaeology Unit, the project undertook community archaeology on three further sites within the city, using a similar approach to public engagement to that used in the Moston scheme. The other sites investigated by Dig Manchester were the post-medieval farm buildings around Wythenshawe Hall, the farm buildings east of the moated Peel Hall (see Dig 5) and the remains of the corn mill at Northenden Mill (Bell, 2009; Garratt, 2009). Between 2004 and 2008 more than thirty schools and 8,000 Manchester residents took part in the project. Such widening participation not only brought new community groupings together but also allowed archaeological sites that were not under the direct threat of redevelopment to be studied and their remains displayed (Nevell, 2013, 67).

The earliest map showing the mill dates from 1641. Later maps from the nineteenth century, particularly the Ordnance Survey maps of the area from 1870s onwards, provided an accurate indication of the location and dimensions of the mill (Bell, 2009, 6–7). Late nineteenth-century photographs indicated the mill structure had two storeys above the river level (Nevell, 2014, 39). The mill was demolished in the 1960s.

The excavation stripped an area of tarmac and gravel in the car park that now occupies the mill site. To the west, next to a row of young trees bordering Mill Lane, a smaller trench was excavated to assess the condition of the mill house. The initial excavation in the car park revealed extensive remains, with handmade brick walls and

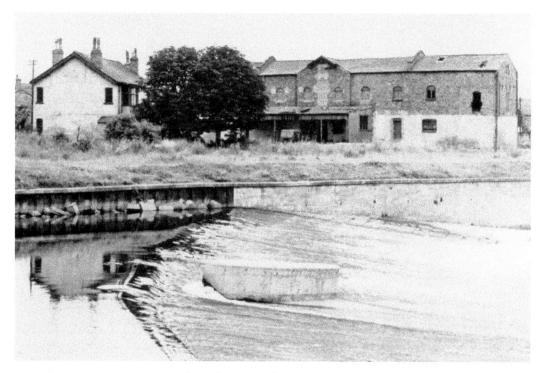

An early twentieth-century view of Northenden Mill across the River Mersey. (Image courtesy of the Greater Manchester Archaeological Advisory Service)

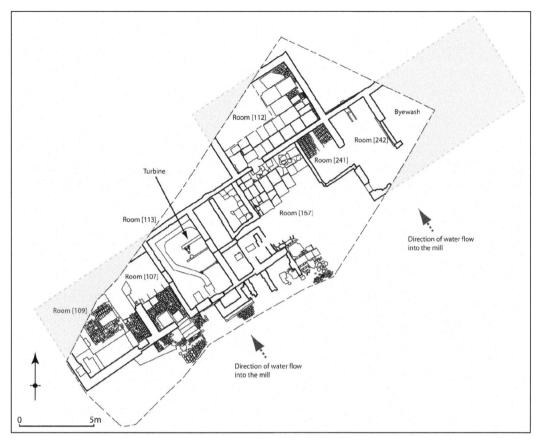

The excavation plan of Northenden Mill. The remains spanned the late seventeenth century to the mid-twentieth century. Throughout that time the site was a water-powered flour mill. (Image courtesy of the Greater Manchester Archaeological Advisory Service)

various types of demolition rubble exposed. The brick walls were interpreted as part of the centre and eastern wing of the mill when compared with the layout of the mill on the Ordnance Survey maps. The depth of the archaeology was also tested and was found to be generally 1 metre deep, but over 2 metres in the area of the wheelpit (Bell, 2009, 4).

During the 2005 excavation a large area of the mill was exposed in Trench 1. This allowed some preliminary dating through the building materials and finds such as pottery and corn drying kiln tiles. The mill walls were mainly constructed from handmade brick dating to the late eighteenth century. However, it soon became evident that the surviving interior of the mill had been radically altered. Most of these modifications dated to the nineteenth and early twentieth centuries. The basement was found to be divided into several separate rooms or compartments. From west to east the mill contained a kiln, a storage room for fuel, a possible wheel pit (later the turbine room), a central storage room with a similar room to the north, a gear room connected to a wheel pit, a byewash channel, and an unexcavated room (Bell, 2009, 24–25).

The western wing contained a kiln that dated to the initial building of the mill. Constructed from handmade brick, the kiln contained a firebox used to heat a floor

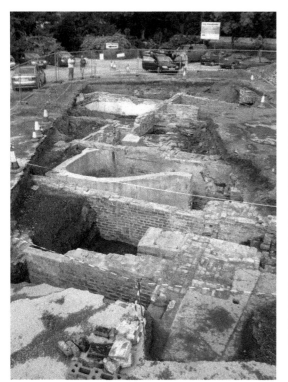

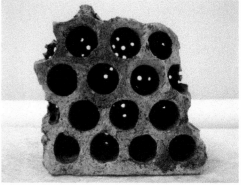

Above: One of the kiln tiles excavated at Northenden Mill. This was part of a structure where grain would have been dried prior to grinding.

Left: The excavations at Northenden Mill, showing the location of the early twentieth-century water turbine (the large concrete oval in the centre of the structure).

situated above the basement level. The early function of the kiln was indicated by the finds from the surrounding rubble. This contained fragments of perforated corn drying kiln tiles. The large flagged central room had few features to indicate its use. The level of this area had been raised over the mill stream so that the building could straddle the stream and channel water through both the culvert and the headrace. Deposits of silt, mud and gravel within this room revealed the amount of flooding that occurred while the building was empty immediately prior to its demolition. The wheel pit and gear room were located at the eastern, river, end of the mill. This area was over 2 metres deep and twin arched outlets in the north wall of the wheel pit were visible. Although the full depth of the wheel pit could not be excavated for reasons of health and safety, the width and type of wheel could be established. Water would have flowed into the southern side of the wheelpit and turned a 5-metre-diameter wheel, before flowing through the stone arches into the tail race. The shaft of the wheel would have been connected to a smaller wheel in the room found immediately to the west. This was the 'pit wheel' and drove a second gear wheel called a 'wallower'. The 'wallower' was connected to an upright shaft and the 'great spur wheel'. This turned the stone spindle which in turn drove the millstone on the floor above (Bell, 2009, 26–29). Limited excavation within the room to the east of the wheel pit suggested that this was used as a byewash channel. This channel would allow the mill stream to flow when the water wheel was not in use. A sluice gate system would have been in use to divert the flow of water to the east of the wheel pit.

It is likely that a second water wheel was located within a room in the western wing of the mill, into which a turbine had been inserted at the end of the nineteenth century. The wheel would have had the same dimensions as that located in the eastern wing, with a diameter of approximately 5 metres. The southern wall of this room contained two arches that linked to the culverted channel running from the Mersey (Bell, 2009, 30).

The excavation at Northenden actively sought to include people of all ages and backgrounds in the archaeological work, with parallel activities involving dig-inspired art for the more artistically inclined, or those unable to dig. On an average week 70–100 adult volunteers and 200–300 schoolchildren would work at the site. During 2006, over the six-week excavation two of the weekends were open for anyone to participate in the excavation. These weekends were primarily aimed at family groups and people who could not take time off during the week to dig. Whole families would spend the day or a half-day on site, with numbers of up to forty people during the busiest days (Nevell, 2014, 39–40). The popularity of the community dig, and the enthusiasm for archaeological work and research shown by the volunteers of southern Manchester, led directly to the formation of local group the South Manchester Archaeological Research Team (SMART).

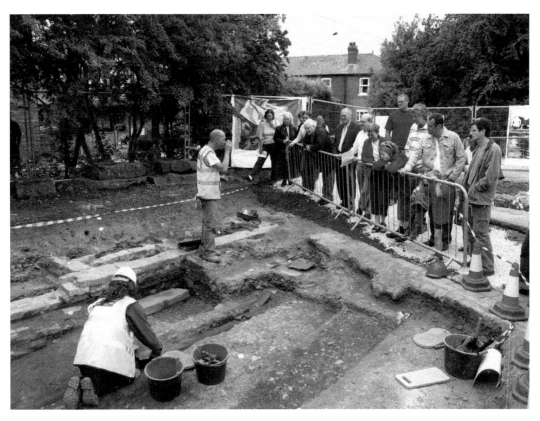

Simon Askew, lead community archaeologist for the Dig Manchester project, leading a public tour of the dig site at Northenden Mill.

Dig 13

The First Mancunians – The Roman Cemetery and Vicus at Great Jackson Street (2007–2008)

In the twenty-first century redevelopment around Castlefield has provided renewed opportunities for investigating the Roman civilian settlement and even the eastern defences of the fort. Perhaps the most significant of these opportunities was the discovery of the first substantial traces of the fort's Roman cemetery on the southern bank of the Medlock, opposite the fort. This work also uncovered an intact Roman altar with the name of one of the first Mancunians – Aelius Sextus.

One aspect of the Roman occupation of Manchester that has remained largely unexplored is the Roman cemetery. In the eighteenth century the city's first historian, John Whitaker, reported that two urns had been found on the southern riverbank of the Medlock opposite the fort (Whitaker, 1773, 59–60). Close by the Chester Road site, in 1821, a group of three sculptured stones were discovered that came from a temple to Mithras. Corbett's map of 1850 notes that Pioneer Quay, which was excavated in 1849, had been part of a Roman cemetery with 'Many Graves and Relics Found'. Apart from urns of 'common red pottery', there was also a cylindrical rock-cut grave (Miller & Cook, 2019, 14).

The site, investigated in February and April 2008 by Pre-Construct Archaeology, lies at the corner of Great Jackson Street and Chester Road. An area covering approximately 43 metres by 57 metres was stripped behind and to the east of the Chester Road frontage and the probable line of the Roman road. Encompassing about 2,200 m², it revealed three phases of Roman activity, much of which was truncated by activity in the late eighteenth, nineteenth and twentieth centuries (Miller & Cook, 2019, 14–16).

The earliest Roman activity took the form of a group of boundary ditches, mostly up to 0.75 metres wide and 0.35 metres deep and ranging from 2.6 metres to 8 metres in length, defining at least three plots of land set out to the south of the Roman road. Although the internal areas of these plots were truncated by later activity, a group of relatively well-preserved features was recorded within the south-eastern corner of the

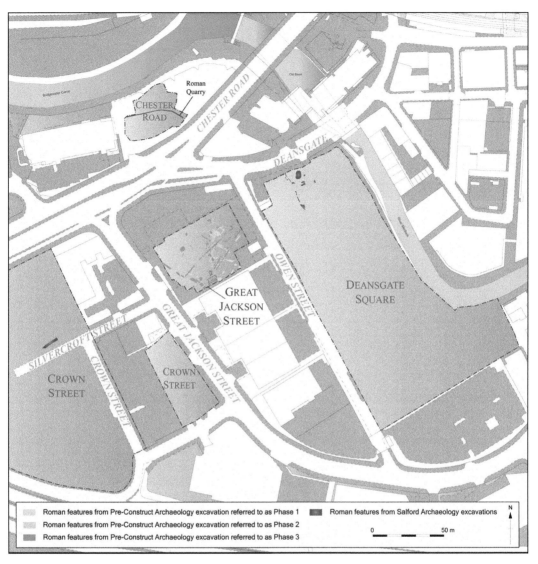

Plan of the Roman excavations undertaken on the southern side of the River Medlock in Manchester between 2008 and 2018.

northernmost plot. They were rubbish pits, and probably initially dug to extract sand, gravel and clay prior to being used for waste disposal (PCA, 2009). Pottery recovered from the plot boundaries and internal features indicates this activity occurred during the early to mid-second century AD. Although no direct evidence of buildings was identified from this phase, the domestic refuse within the rubbish pits implied nearby habitation. It thus seems likely that during the second century dwellings and shops lined the Roman road to the north, and that their back yards were used for rubbish disposal activities (PCA, 2009, 20–25).

The second phase of Roman activity saw the reordering of this part of the settlement. The small regular plots were replaced by a more substantial boundary system. A single

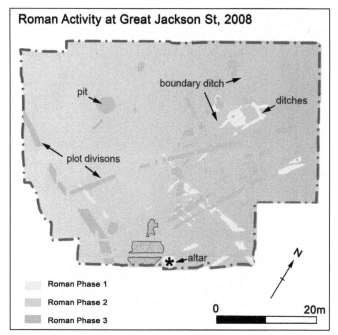

Roman Activity at Great Jackson St, 2008

pit

boundary ditch

ditches

plot divisons

* altar

N

Roman Phase 1
Roman Phase 2
Roman Phase 3

0   20m

Left: Plan of the Roman features excavated at the Great Jackson Street site in 2008 by Pre-Construct Archaeology, showing the location of the altar.

Below: Some of the early second-century plot ditches excavated at Jackson Street on the south side of the River Medlock. (Image courtesy of the Greater Manchester Archaeological Advisory Service)

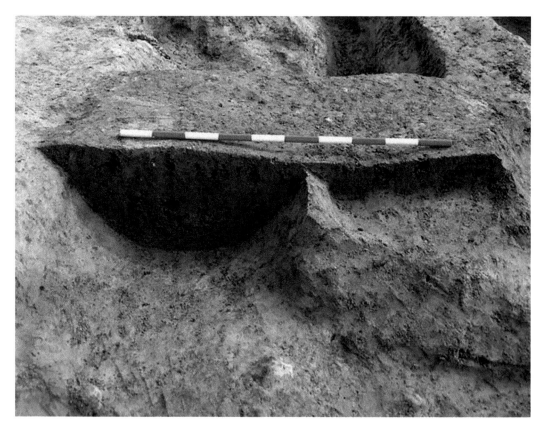

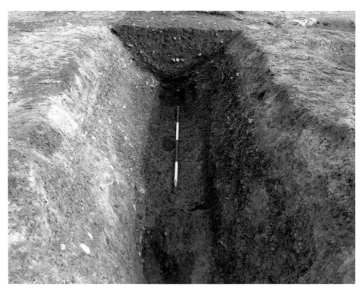

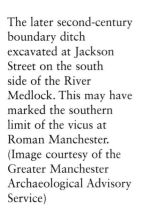

The later second-century boundary ditch excavated at Jackson Street on the south side of the River Medlock. This may have marked the southern limit of the vicus at Roman Manchester. (Image courtesy of the Greater Manchester Archaeological Advisory Service)

ditch running west to east was traced for more than 17 metres and was 2 metres wide and over 1 metre deep. There were traces of a wooden box drain with lead fittings at its base. Pottery recovered from this ditch and other features dates this activity to the late second century AD (PCA, 2009, 25–26).

The final Roman phase of activity saw a further change in the layout of the site. A third set of shallower boundaries and eight plots were laid out. Within these plots were beam slots and postholes, although no clear building plans were recovered. Clusters of rubbish pits yielded domestic refuse that indicate nearby habitation. A substantial ditch bounding the south-western side of these plots might mark the limit of the extramural settlement during this period. The pottery recovered from this phase suggests an early to mid-third-century date (PCA, 2009, 26–34).

Thereafter, the site was abandoned and the Roman remains were overlain by a plough soil, up to 0.5 metres thick, suggesting long agricultural use. It was not until the late eighteenth century, when the area became part of the booming industrial town of Manchester, that the site began to be built upon (Miller & Cook, 2019, 24–27).

The most striking Roman object from the site was discovered in a large pit in the southernmost plot. This quarry pit had been back-filled with an inscribed altar and a fine piece of Samian bowl depicting a hunting scene. The altar was probably set up as a roadside shrine and was presumably disposed of in the pit when obsolete. Inscriptions from the Roman fort in Manchester have been recorded since the early seventeenth century, but this find is only the third Roman altar located in Manchester and the first since 1832.

The altar takes the form of a column with larger base and capital. It is about 970 mm tall with a maximum width of 375 mm and a depth of 255 mm. On top of the capital is a small circular dish-shaped area, the focus for offerings, which is framed by two bolsters decorated at the front. The tool marks made by a claw chisel and a flat chisel are clearly visible on the sides of the altar.

The text reads: DEABVS / MATRIBVS / HANANEFTIS / ET OLLOTOTIS / AELIVS / VICTOR / V S L L M.

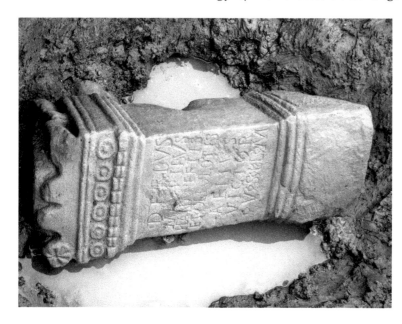

The Roman altar set up by Aelius Victor *in situ* in a later second-century rubbish pit at Jackson Street in 2008. Aelius Victor is only the second named individual associated with Roman Manchester. (Image courtesy of the Greater Manchester Archaeological Advisory Service)

This has been translated by Dr Paul Holder (PCA, 2009, 69–71) as: 'To the mother goddesses Hananeftae and to the mother goddesses Ollototae, Aelius Victor gladly, willingly, and deservedly fulfilled his vow.'

The discovery confirms the eighteenth and nineteenth-century antiquarian evidence for a group of shrines along the Roman road to Chester. It names two groups of mother goddesses. According to Paul Holder the matres Ollototae have only been recorded in Britain, whereas the matres Hananeftae have been recorded from altars in Cologne in Germania Inferior. Both represent the mother goddesses of the Cannanefatian tribe from this area. Aelius Victor, the dedicant, by choosing to honour the matres Hananeftae was therefore most likely a Cannanefatian (PCA, 2009, 69–71).

The archaeological context of the find indicates a date after the middle of the second century for the production of the altar and its disposal. This matches the information to be gleaned from the text and from similar finds, and it seems likely that it was made no later than the AD 230s (Holder 20??). There is no unit named on the altar, but again it seems likely that Aelius Victor had either served in the army or was still a soldier at the time of the altar's dedication. At this period, usually only the military could afford or want to commission an altar to fulfil a vow.

Further evidence for Roman activity on the southern bank of the Medlock was located immediately north-east of this site at Deansgate Square in 2016 (Miller & Cook, 2019, 17–19). This took the form of ditched plot boundaries and evidence for cremation activity, although no burials were located. This fresh evidence confirmed what had been uncovered at Great Jackson Street in 2008: that the vicus extended along Chester Road south of the river crossing of the Medlock for several hundred metres, probably as a discrete suburb, and beyond this was the settlement's cemetery. The site supplied only the second named individual from Roman Manchester, and the first to be discovered for nearly four centuries.

Dig 14

Hell on Earth – Loom Street Housing and the Ancoats Slums (2007)

The early twenty-first-century redevelopment of Manchester provided an opportunity to investigate some of the most notorious workers' housing and associated slums in nineteenth-century Britain. One of these areas was Ancoats, noted by social commentators such as Frederick Engels and Elizabeth Gaskell as one of the worst areas of slum housing in Manchester. Since 2001 archaeological work has been targeting the excavation of workers' housing from the eighteenth and nineteenth centuries. Over forty sites have been looked at and the remains of several hundred houses excavated or, more rarely, recorded as standing structures. Most of the excavations of workers' housing in Manchester record few individual properties. Excavations by the University of Manchester along Loom Street in Ancoats during the autumn of 2007 exposed forty-six dwellings and showed for the first time how such extensive excavations could reveal the detailed history of individual properties and their occupants (Gregory, 2007c; Nevell, 2008, 152–59).

Seven area excavations in a block of land either side of Loom Street, bounded by George Leigh, Bengal, Sherratt and Blossom Streets (Areas A to G), exposed the partial or complete floor plans of forty-six dwellings (Gregory, 2007c). This represents one of the largest archaeological investigations of late eighteenth, nineteenth and early twentieth-century workers' housing within the city.

The largest of the properties excavated were found fronting George Leigh Street and were exposed during the excavation of Area A and Area D. These properties measured around 5.5 metres wide (Houses D2–3) close to the corner of George Leigh Street and Bengal Street, narrowing to around 4.7 metres wide further along George Leigh Street (House D3 & A1). Each of the properties was provided with half-basements and raised ground floors. The properties (Houses B1–2, B4–5) found close to the corner of Loom and Sherratt Street were slightly smaller in size, measuring 4.5 metres wide by 7 metres deep. These properties differed in one major respect – they did not have basements. The houses (Houses E1–3) excavated at the eastern end of Loom Street were smaller in size and were probably of lower status than the eighteenth-century houses fronting Loom Street and George Leigh Street. As with the larger properties found at the western end

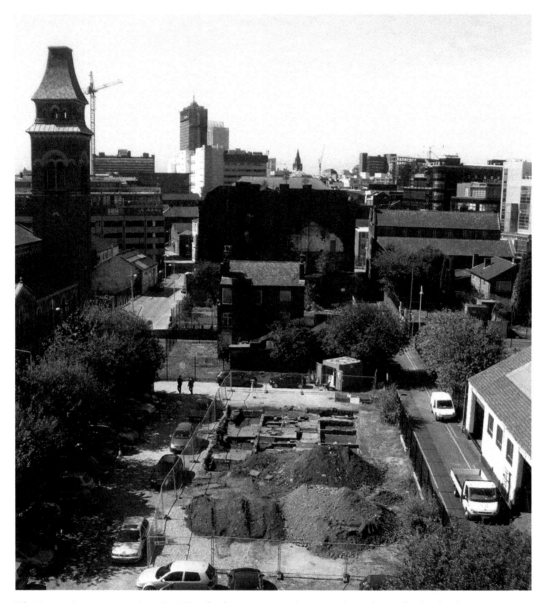

The Loom Street excavations in 2007, looking westwards across the industrial suburb of Ancoats towards the city centre. Ancoats was Manchester's industrial powerhouse in the late eighteenth and early nineteenth century and was the focus of steam-powered cotton spinning, manufacture and engineering production.

of Loom Street, these properties did not have basements. The remains indicate that each house measured 4 metres wide by 6.5 metres deep, comprising a rear room around 2.8 metres deep and a larger 3.7-metre-deep front room. Within the rear room of the properties were fireplaces and flights of stairs giving access to the first floor (Gregory, 2007c; Nevell, 2019).

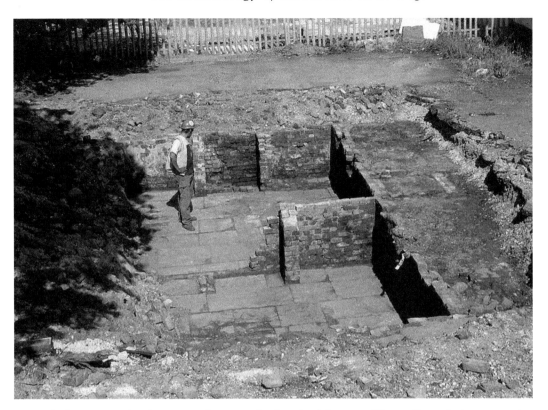

The basements of early nineteenth-century back-to-back houses off Loom Street during excavation in 2007 by the University of Manchester Archaeological Unit.

The most common house type excavated at Loom Street was the back-to-back dwelling. The earliest examples were constructed between 1787–94 and 1818–19 and fronted both George Leigh Street and Jepson's Court, but were accessed from Loom Street. These houses had half-basements that contained fireplaces on their eastern walls. One property (House C2) measured internally 4.1 metres by 4 metres, whilst another (House C1) measured 3.9 metres by 3.9 metres. Access into the individual basements was via ladders leading from a trap door, which opened at ground level within each of the dwellings above. There was no evidence for cellar lights for the properties found fronting Jepson's Court, indicating that if these basements were occupied the living conditions would have been particularly oppressive as they were not lit by natural light or have adequate ventilation.

These properties represent a microcosm of the early to mid-nineteenth-century urban development within Manchester. During the early nineteenth century the population expansion of the city led to vacant areas between the established housing stock being infilled with new worker's dwellings, which were often back-to-back and blind-back properties accessed only by narrow alleyways. This period also saw a more intensive occupation of the older housing stock, with the creation of cellar dwellings. As a result, Ancoats's population steadily increased from 11,039 in 1801 to 55,983 in 1861 (Roberts, 1993, 16). This period of increased housing pressure was followed in the later nineteenth century by a slow improvement in housing quality through the addition of back yard privies, the closure of cellar dwellings and the demolition of some of the worst type of housing (Nevell, 2018).

The work at Loom Street demonstrated the problems of dealing with fragmentary artefactual evidence from an area with both a highly mobile population and extensive later rebuilding. The forty-six dwellings investigated produced 1,024 finds, representing 768 individual items. Of these the ceramic assemblage amounted to 779 individual stratified fragments of pottery, representing a minimum estimated number of 527 pottery vessels, weighing 23.664 kg. The ceramic material falls into two broad groups according to period: post-medieval (pre-1800) pottery and industrially produced ceramics of the nineteenth and early twentieth centuries. The ceramic assemblage can be sub-divided further into fine tableware and utilitarian coarse wares. Only a small percentage of the assemblage could be directly associated with the structural remains of late eighteenth- and nineteenth-century worker's housing. Most of the artefacts were derived from secondary contexts associated with later demolition and infilling episodes and dated to the later nineteenth and early twentieth centuries.

The Loom Street assemblage, both fine ware and coarse ware types of ceramic, shows a remarkable restricted range of forms and decorative treatment, with most ceramic products being manufactured in Manchester and Staffordshire, though a few stoneware bottles were manufactured in Bristol and Glasgow. There was a great degree of repetition of styles within the ceramic groups recovered. This could be the result of demolition spreads of material containing fragments from the same vessel (as was seen in Area C House C2 and Area D House D1) or because the domestic ceramic repertoires of the nineteenth-century inhabitants were utilising standard contemporary items that were easily accessible and affordable. The overall emphasis in the assemblage on fine wares as opposed to coarse wares suggested that previously utilitarian products, such as brown stoneware and dark-glazed coarse wares, were being replaced by cheaper white wares, such as polychrome-banded factory-produced slipware, used in the pantry, dairy or kitchen for cold storage.

In terms of local migration, the existence of jumbled fragments of mismatched pottery was noted in just a few of the houses along Loom Street. This may reflect the local movement of transient individuals and families where some items are abandoned whilst others are taken to the new home. Notable small groupings came from dwellings in Areas D and G, which produced two fragments of Black Basalt Ware. Jepson's Court (Area C) produced thirty-nine fragments, including twenty-nine sherds that represented fragments of earthenware, stoneware and white ware bottles, jars, jugs and saucers. Area D 1, House 1, also produced fragmentary ceramic remains from a drain, representing a cup and saucer.

The Loom Street excavations provide evidence for the daily routines of household life, particularly around cleaning and food preparation, as well as the changing housing conditions of the industrial city. This evidence is a reminder that the industrial archaeology of Manchester is about more than just its manufacturing industries. The Loom Street evidence helped to justify the decision of the city's planning archaeologists in the late 1990s to target the excavation of these domestic sites.

Dig 15

Jersey Street Court Housing, Ancoats (2011)

Ancoats was part of the city infamous for the poor quality of its industrial period housing jammed between the cotton mills, iron works and warehouses. Excavation of this row of early nineteenth-century courtyard housing on the corner of Jersey Street and Pickford Street revealed an unusually large quantity of pottery, glass and metalwork revealing details of the city's market networks (Nevell, 2017, 10–11).

The corner of Jersey Street and Pickford lies at the north-western edge of Ancoats, just behind Great Ancoats Street. This former industrial suburb has seen a huge amount of redevelopment activity in the early twenty-first century, with the conversion of a number of cotton mills, but excavation work ahead of new housing has revealed remains such as the Percival Vickers glass works (see Dig 10). At Jersey Street eight dwellings from a set of ten back-to-backs forming Hall's Court were excavated in 2011 by the Centre for Applied Archaeology at the University of Salford. These dwellings were built in a single phase between 1794 and 1800, making them amongst the earliest known examples of this building type in Manchester. The buildings were finally demolished in 1970, further

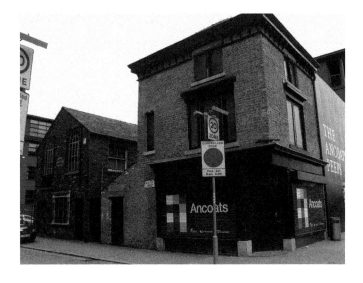

Surviving early nineteenth-century housing on the corner of Jersey Street and Great Ancoats Street in the early twenty-first century.

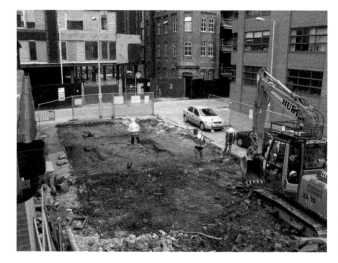

The excavated remains of the back-to-back housing known at Hall's Court, on the corner of Jersey Street and Pickford Street. This type of housing typified the city's early nineteenth-century housing stock.

enhancing their importance within Ancoats, as this arrangement of dwellings set around a narrow courtyard (known by contemporaries as 'court housing') spans almost the full history of the industrial suburb (Cattell & Nevell, 2011; Nevell, 2014, 54–56).

The houses are shown in detail on Banck's map of Manchester from 1830. A passageway ran from the eastern side of Jersey Street to give access to the southern row of five back-to-backs. The other side of the passageway was occupied by a school. Hall's Court comprised a block of ten two-storey, back-to-back properties forming Nos 1 to 7 Hall's Court to the south, Nos 4 and 6 Jersey Street to the west and Nos 2 to 8 Pickford Street to the north. Frederick Engels in his commentary on Ancoats noted that the construction of the workers' houses in the area around Jersey Street was '... on closer examination ... evident that the walls of these cottages are as thin as it is possible to make them. The outer walls, those of the cellar, which bear the weight of the ground-floor and roof, are one whole brick thick at most ...' (Engels, 1845). The properties forming Hall's Court were not cellared, nor were the outer walls of the house foundations just a single brick thick. These properties were, then, somewhat superior to those elsewhere on Jersey Street (Nevell, 2017, 10).

After minor alterations in the mid-nineteenth century, during the 1880s (identified in the excavations as Phase 3) the buildings at Hall's Court were substantially redeveloped. Goad's Insurance Map of Manchester from 1888 shows that Nos 4 and 6 Jersey Street were extended by knocking through into Nos 1 and 3 Hall's Court and into No. 2 Pickford Street to create two larger commercial premises that functioned as a hairdressers and general provisions store. No. 5 Hall's Court appeared to have been demolished and replaced by a single-storey outbuilding and yard. No. 7 Hall's Court also appears to have been demolished and in its place was a single-storey rear extension to No. 8 Pickford Street. No. 4 Pickford Street was demolished and replaced by a single-storey structure with a front yard, possibly serving as an outbuilding for the expanded No. 6 Jersey Street. Whilst Nos 6 and 8 Pickford Street were knocked through to create one larger dwelling.

Documentary and cartographic sources from the nineteenth century confirmed Nos 4 and 6 Jersey Street functioned as commercial premises but had living accommodation on the upper floors. In contrast, Nos 1 to 7 Hall's Court and Nos 2 to 10 Pickford Street

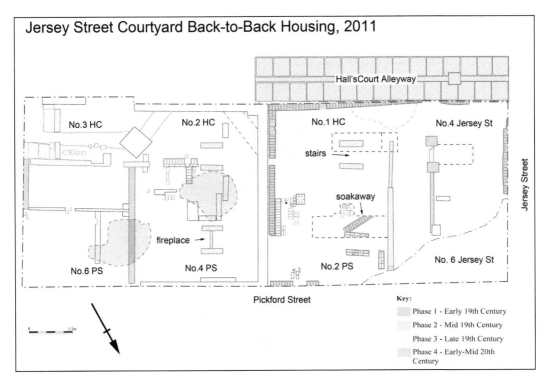

An excavated plan of the courtyard back-to-back housing at Jersey Street, explored in 2011 by the University of Salford. Key: HC refers to Hall's Court and PS refers to Pickford Street.

were all private dwellings. Census returns and trade directories from the period 1797 to 1881 have established that these properties were occupied by local mill workers (cotton piercers and weavers, almost all in Hall's Court in the period 1851–81) and artisans and tradespeople (barbers, boatman, chair maker, coffee mill maker, dress maker, glaziers, fishmonger, greengrocer, hairdresser, joiner's assistant, plaster's labourer, plumbers, provisions dealer, shoemaker, sugar boiler, warehouse worker, a washer woman and even a lawyer). One of the reasons for so many trades was the regular turnover of tenants in Hall's Court and along Pickford Street. Nos 4 and 6 Jersey Street saw longer term tenants, such as James Hardman, hairdresser (1879–1920), at No. 4. The Census Returns from 1891 and 1901 indicated that Hall's Court had ceased to be used as dwellings and were uninhabited. Twentieth-century Census Returns, rate books and trade directories from the period 1901 to 1961 indicate that Nos 4 and 6 Jersey Street, whilst in use as commercial dwellings, continued to have dwellings in the upper storeys (Phase 4) (Nevell, 2017, 11).

The excavations produced a closely stratified group of pottery found in drainage and levelling layers associated with three of the main phases of the buildings. Most of the artefacts were derived from primary and secondary contexts, dating to the nineteenth century and early twentieth century. A small proportion (some black-glazed finewares and some of the cream wares) were dateable to the late eighteenth/early nineteenth century when the houses were built. The single largest category of objects was pottery, eighty-one sherds, mainly from three contexts: two dumping levels and a make-up levelling layer all associated with Phases 2 and 3 of the complex (broadly mid to late nineteenth century).

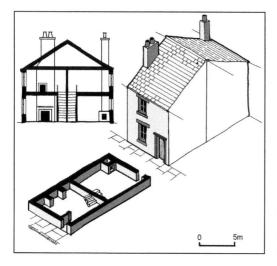

A suggested reconstruction of the pair of back-to-back houses, No. 1 Hall's Court and No. 2 Pickford Street, as excavated in 2011.

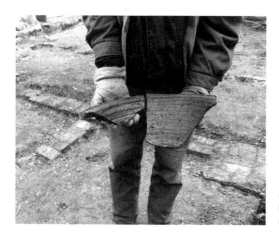

An early nineteenth-century glazed earthenware bowl excavated from the floor of No. 2 Pickford Street, Ancoats.

This ceramic material formed seventeen black-gazed earthenware vessels, nine cream ware vessels, five brown stoneware vessels, one dark-glazed fineware vessel and one unglazed earthenware vessel. These were mostly bowls and jars, although there were at least one cream ware plate and one cream ware jug. Of particular note was a pair of pince-nez, excavated from a Phase 2 deposit (early to mid-nineteenth-century) in No. 6 Pickford Street, occupied by the Chapman and Eagle families in the mid-nineteenth century. No. 4 Jersey Street, occupied by the Hardman family from the 1870s into the early twentieth century, produced a clearance group (from the Phase 2 levelling context 27) that might be associated with the Hardmans. This included utilitarian earthenware used in the kitchen or dairy, stoneware vessels used in the pantry or cellar for cold storage, and fine porcelains and whitewares used at the table (Nevell, 2017, 11).

The ceramic assemblage from Jersey Street provides an invaluable insight into the nineteenth-century domestic repertoire from working class dwellings at the heart of the industrial core of industrial Manchester. Its importance lies in the social history it records, through the material possessions of the residents

Dig 16

Excavating John Ashbury's Carriage & Iron Works, Gorton (2012 and 2014)

Manchester became a leading centre for machine tool, textile machinery and locomotive manufacture during the nineteenth century. The concentration of a large number of textile mills all requiring engineering infrastructure (in the form of line-shafting, boilers and steam engines) encouraged the growth of iron founding and machine manufacture in the city from the 1790s onwards. The development of the city as a railway hub in the 1830s and 1840s cemented Manchester's position as an engineering centre of excellence (Nevell, 2018, 35). Yet the mid-twentieth-century decline of engineering left very few traces of the city's engineering legacy. Ashbury's, founded during the 1830s in Gorton, was one of the biggest of the new railway engineering works established in the mid-nineteenth century in Manchester. Its excavation in 2012 and 2014 through the planning process by SLR Consulting Ltd and Oxford Archaeology North, and funded by Network Rail and PP Plasma Limited, was the first time such a works had been studied in this way within the city. It revealed extensive evidence for a variety of iron working processes that were not previously recorded archaeologically (Hayes, 2014, 2–5; Nevell, 2018, 35–39). The fact the site was excavated by two separate archaeology contractors, funded by two separate developers two years apart, reflected the way in which the regeneration of Manchester and the funding of developer-led archaeology work now functioned in the early twenty-first-century city.

Manchester's engineering sector began with the arrival of mechanised textile production. Amongst the first generation of firms was Galloway, Bowman & Glasgow. William Galloway senior (1768–1836) was a Scottish engineer who moved from London to Manchester in 1806, teaming up with James Bowman. The new firm worked from the Caledonian Foundry in Great Bridgewater Street as millwrights and engineers. The company became known for its boilers and mill engines. Peel & Williams, engineers and millwrights, was another first-generation engineering company, founded by George Peel (1774–1810) and William Ward Williams (1772–1833) around 1800. They were iron founders, engineers and roller manufacturers producing steam engines and textile machinery. Their first factory was in Miller Street though later factories were in Ancoats: the Phoenix Foundry was established around 1804 on Swan Street and the

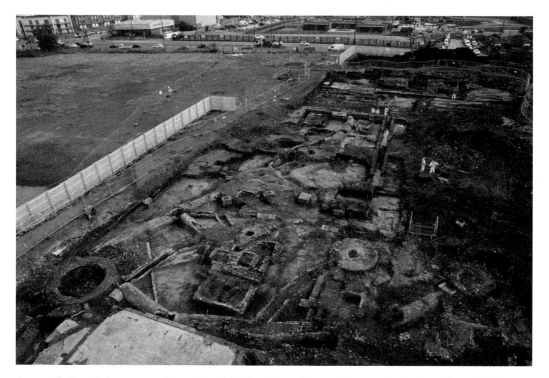

An aerial view of the excavated remains of Ashbury's carriage and iron works in Openshaw, 2012, showing the flues and furnace bases from the mid to late nineteenth century. (Image courtesy of the Greater Manchester Archaeological Advisory Service)

Soho Foundry of around 1810 lay on Pollard Street. This was a trend that many of the 100 iron founders established in the city by 1850 followed and the industrial suburbs of Ancoats and Gorton became a focus for engineering firms, encouraged by access to coal along the Ashton and Rochdale canals built through the area in the 1790s, new turnpike roads and, from the 1830s, by the arrival of the railways.

Amongst the first generation of railway engineering firms established within Manchester to service the new railway infrastructure was the Ashbury Railway Carriage & Iron Company Ltd. This was originally founded in 1847 by John Ashbury (1806–66) on Commercial Street in Deansgate in the engineering quarter that grew up around Knott Mill. As with many early engineers, in order to expand sites had to be found elsewhere in Manchester. After moving to Ardwick in 1844, another site in Openshaw was developed from 1847 and by 1860 the firm was employing 1,700 people, making it one of the larger engineering employers in the city. The firm specialised in producing railway rolling stock, locomotive components and wagon repairs for the Manchester, Sheffield & Lincolnshire Railway. Like many other engineering works in the early 1830s, they also built several locomotives for the Liverpool & Manchester Railway. They supplied 6,000 wagons for the building of the Manchester Ship Canal in the later 1880s and early 1890s, being able to produce 100 wagons and ten railway carriages per week at this time. Taken over in 1919, the site was closed in 1928.

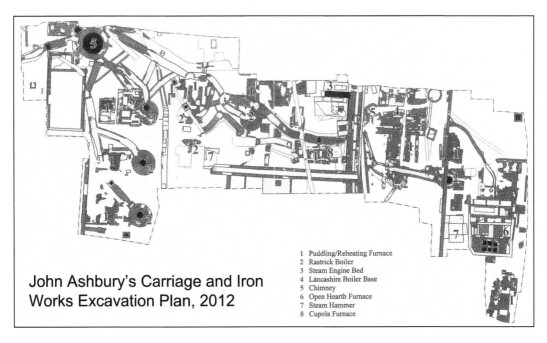

John Ashbury's Carriage and Iron Works Excavation Plan, 2012

1 Puddling/Reheating Furnace
2 Rastrick Boiler
3 Steam Engine Bed
4 Lancashire Boiler Base
5 Chimney
6 Open Hearth Furnace
7 Steam Hammer
8 Cupola Furnace

Detailed excavation plan of the various furnaces uncovered at Ashbury's carriage and iron works in 2012 by SLR Consulting. (Image courtesy of the Greater Manchester Archaeological Advisory Service)

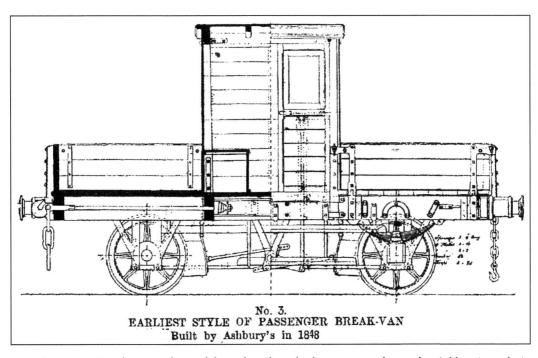

No. 3.
EARLIEST STYLE OF PASSENGER BREAK-VAN
Built by Ashbury's in 1848

An engineering drawing of one of the early railway brake vans manufactured at Ashbury's works in the 1840s and 1850s. (Image courtesy of the Greater Manchester Archaeological Advisory Service)

A large element of the firm's 6.7-hectare works in Openshaw was excavated in 2012 and 2014. The most complex part of the works was that investigated in 2012 by SLR Consulting. This was the foundry section of the works, where remains of the full sequence of iron and steel production technologies of the site's eighty-one-year history were recovered. The dig recovered the extensive remains of nine puddling or reverberatory furnaces (around 3 metres by 6 metres) for making wrought iron, eight Rastrick boilers used to recover heat from the exhaust gases produced by the puddling furnaces, the bases of three cupola furnaces (each around 3 metres by 5 metres), associated brick flues and chimneys, an open hearth for making steel and a steam hammer (Hayes, 2014, 22–24). Wrought iron was manufactured on site using the puddling furnaces from the 1840s onwards, with steel being introduced in the 1890s, the single open hearth replacing the nine puddling furnaces. The foundry had open sides to allow air to pass through freely and the furnaces were arranged around the northern, western and eastern sides, close to the air. Although not excavated, in the southern part of the building were a set of steam-powered rollers for shaping the iron products, a steam engine and Lancashire boiler excavated on the eastern side of the trench probably powering these rollers.

After the Ashbury's works was merged with the Metropolitan Amalgamated Railway Carriage Wagon Company Limited in 1902, this part of the works was redesigned (Hayes, 2014, 35–6). The foundry was demolished and a new erecting shed with a travelling crane, the stone foundations of which were located, was built and used to make parts for the carriages and wagons. The 2014 dig site immediately to the north explored the large engineering and assembly shops, with their travelling cranes, brick floors and railway sidings that included a carriage turntable 4.3 metres wide (Hayes, 2014, 44–45).

In total 7,600 m² or just 11 per cent of the 6.7-hectare site was excavated in the two digs, though this does make it one the biggest excavation sites so far investigated archaeologically in the early twenty-first-century city. One further point is worthy of mention. The 2012 dig site was also notable for the co-operation and close working relationship between the professional archaeologists of SLR Consulting and the members of the Manchester Regional Industrial Archaeology Society. The specialist industrial archaeology knowledge of the local archaeology society was used to help the professional archaeologist interpret some of the more complex power and furnace systems, demonstrating the continued value of co-operation between professional and volunteer archaeologists.

Dig 17

Dig Greater Manchester: Hulme Barracks and the Peterloo Massacre (2013)

The community archaeology projects of the early twenty-first century were succeeded by Dig Greater Manchester, one of the largest community archaeology projects of the early 2010s in Britain. Running from 2011 to 2016, and led by a team of three community archaeologists from the University of Salford (Brian Grimsditch, Sarah Cattell and Vicky Nash), it engaged 1,588 adult volunteers, 2,409 open day visitors, and 3,406 school children, as well as delivering 116 training workshops and 66 lectures across 11 local authorities, which produced two conferences and two major publications (Nevell, 2019, 77). As the successor to both I Dig Moston and Dig Manchester, the Dig Greater Manchester project aimed to provide community archaeology education and training across the Manchester city region; to explore the impact of community archaeology on participating individuals, local groups, and communities; and to explore the impact of industrialisation in the region. This was done through excavating eleven sites in Greater Manchester and one in Blackburn and Darwen Council. All these sites were on local council land and ranged from textile mill workers' housing to factory owners' houses and a cavalry barracks. A key site was Hulme Barracks, where the remains of the cavalry base that was used during the Peterloo massacre were uncovered (Thompson, 2015, 152–3).

Barracks Park in Hulme was chosen as the Dig Greater Manchester community archaeology site for the city, partly because it was on open land owned by the city council, but also because it was a site associated with the Peterloo Massacre of 1819. On 16 August 1819 around 60,000 campaigners gathered on St Peter's Fields in Manchester (roughly the area between the present Free Trade Hall and St Peter's Square) to demand Parliamentary reform. Trouble began when the yeomanry tried to arrest the speakers at the rally. The crowd panicked and the hussars were then ordered to make a sabre charge in an effort to restore order. That charge left up to fifteen dead and around 700 injured. And the term Peterloo? That was used to mock the soldiers at Manchester by echoing Waterloo. The soldiers from that battle, which ended the Napoleonic Wars in 1815, were seen by many as heroes for helping save Britain from totalitarian rule, so such a jibe was two-edged: the 15th King's Hussars had fought at Waterloo, and their actions in 1819 were verging on the totalitarian intolerance the battle had been fought for (Kidd & Wyke, 2016, 205–208).

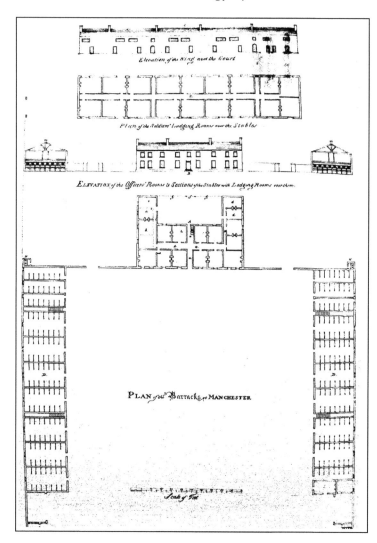

A mid-nineteenth-century plan of Hulme cavalry barracks. The hussars based here in 1819 provided the cavalry that helped police the public meeting at Peters Fields that ended in the Peterloo Massacre.

The massacre was widely condemned at the time and remembered in Percy Bysshe Shelley's political poem *The Masque of Anarchy*. It has been described by some historians as a world-changing event and it has been claimed that it led to the rise of the Chartist Movement (from which grew trade unions) and even that it resulted in the establishment of the *Manchester Guardian* and ultimately helped pave the way towards ordinary people being given the vote (Poole, 2012, 1–5).

Barracks Park was the site of Hulme Barracks, a cavalry barracks in use from 1804 to 1915, and the base of the 15th King's Hussars. The site housed up to 399 hussars and twenty officers at the height of its use in 1839. It was established at a time of war (against France) and its location on the southern edge of the most famous manufacturing town in Britain was also a statement about the worry such a large urban population, the largest outside London, could pose to the Government of the day. The buildings stopped being a cavalry barracks in 1895 and were used by infantry battalions before it was

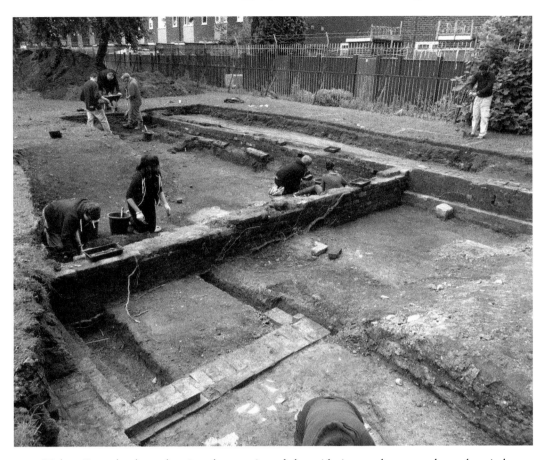

Hulme Barracks, here showing the remains of the mid-nineteenth-century horse hospital, was excavated as part of the Dig Greater Manchester community archaeology project, in July 2013, by the University of Salford.

The excavation of the barracks boundary wall and adjacent workers' housing and roadway. Many of the cavalry veterans settled in the houses around the barracks site in the mid-nineteenth century.

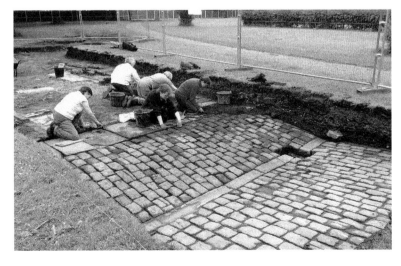

sold to the Manchester Corporation in 1915. The corporation demolished the majority of the site but kept the now Grade II listed officers' quarters and mess, which was used as a bowling green clubhouse before being handed to the St George's Community Association (Nevell, 2019, 34–36).

There had been no building work on the site since it was demolished, most of the area becoming a park. Thus, the excavations were able to uncover undisturbed deposits from the nineteenth century. Four trenches were positioned to target the site's barracks, canteen, riding school and terraced houses. The excavation of the remains of the barracks (two-storey structures with ground-floor stables and living accommodation accessed from a long veranda) was made difficult by later tree planting, but the other three trenches all produced significant remains. The foundations of the original brick perimeter wall of the barracks were found in several locations and in one area back-to-back houses were found to abut this wall. These early nineteenth-century houses were occupied by retired hussars and the Census Returns from the mid-nineteenth century show how the houses around the barracks had become an ex-soldiers' colony (Nevell, 2019, 35–36).

The site produced large quantities of material from the canteen area, and around the barracks and workers' housing. This material culture included pottery and glass bottles from throughout the nineteenth century, as well as buttons from military uniforms and other items that could be directly linked to the hussars who occupied the site. Amongst the most domestic items were a number of single-shot bottles of the beef extract drink Bovril found along with clay pipes and uniform buttons at Hulme Barracks. First made in 1871, the drink was originally known as Johnston's Fluid Beef before being renamed in 1886. They may have been issued to the hussars in their rations and probably formed a welcome hot drink on a cold Manchester winter's night (Nevell, 2019, 34–36).

These remains provide, for the first time, physical evidence to illustrate the human side of the story of the hussars in the early nineteenth century. The survival of the barracks throughout that century reflected both the continuing worries of successive governments and also Manchester's role as a recruitment ground for the army. They are also a timely reminder (the 200th anniversary of the massacre was in 2019) that archaeology has the ability to produce new evidence beyond the textile factory and the cellar dwelling about this important period when the world's first industrial city was emerging.

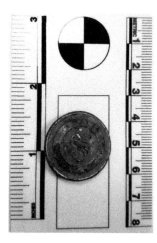

A cavalry uniform button of the mid-nineteenth century, excavated at Hulme Barracks.

Dig 18

Manchester's First Cotton Mill – Arkwright's Shudehill Mill (2005 and 2014–2015)

The first purpose-built cotton spinning mill in Manchester was erected by Sir Richard Arkwright in 1781–83. This was a building so revolutionary that there were protests and demonstrations against its construction. The excavation of this mill, first in 2005 and later in 2014 to 2015, demonstrated the revolutionary nature of this site, with five phases of steam engine design spanning the 1780s to the 1810s, and the discovery of the remains of Manchester's first mill chimney.

Arkwright's Shudehill Mill lies on the northern edge of the Georgian boom town, between Miller Street and Angel Street. Begun in 1781, it was converted to warehousing in the late nineteenth century and destroyed by bombing during the Manchester Blitz of December 1940. The site was first excavated in 2005 by Channel 4's *Time Team* television archaeology programme. Redevelopment in the 2010s by the land-owners, the Co-operative Group, led to the whole site being stripped and excavated in 2014 to 2015 by Oxford Archaeology North (Miller & Wild, 2015, 22–25).

Manchester's role as the centre of global mechanised cotton manufacture and marketing in the nineteenth century has long been studied. Yet it was not until the 1980s that attention turned to recording the surviving cotton spinning mills within the city and its region. The *Cotton Mills in Greater Manchester* volume was published in 1992 as one of three pioneering studies of standing textile mill buildings in England (Williams with Farnie, 1992; the others cover east Cheshire and Yorkshire). These volumes concentrated on the standing remains of the cotton, silk and woollen factory industries, for which even in the early twenty-first century there are very extensive remains within the Manchester city region, with roughly 400 cotton-related structures surviving. This is less than half the number of standing structures recorded in the late 1980s. Excavation is an increasingly important way of recording and understanding the development of the textile mill in the eighteenth, nineteenth and twentieth centuries (Nevell, 2011, 153–56; Nevell, 2018, 14–17). This was first demonstrated within the Manchester city region by the evaluation excavation and then area excavation of Manchester's first purpose-built cotton spinning mill, Arkwright's Shudehill Mill.

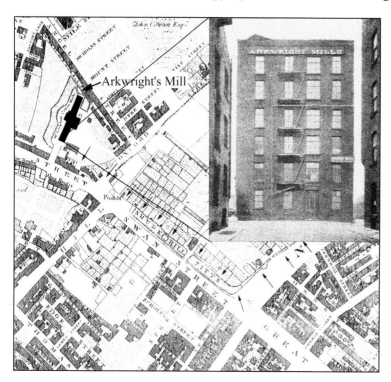

The location of Arkwright's Shudehill Mill, Manchester's first purpose-built cotton spinning mill, erected in 1781–83. Here it is shown on Greene's map of Manchester, published in 1794 along with the earliest photograph of the site.

Sir Richard Arkwright (1732–92), working with clockmaker John Kay, had succeeded in producing a machine capable of spinning cotton yarn, which he patented in 1769. This became known as the waterframe once it had been adapted so that it could be powered by a waterwheel. In 1771 he built a water-powered cotton spinning mill at Cromford, Derbyshire, to house this new technology. In 1775 he secured a patent for a rotary carding machine, a key part of the preparatory process for spinning cotton which transformed the raw cotton into a cotton lap (rather like cotton wool) that was then suitable for spinning. By 1785, when Arkwright's patents were revoked, over 150 cotton spinning mills had been built in Britain using his designs and system of working. This marked the birth of the industrial factory system (Nevell, 2008). Arkwright's Manchester cotton mill was part of a building programme that saw him establish mills in Derbyshire, Lancashire, Nottinghamshire and Scotland. Manchester, as the centre of the cotton trade, was an ideal place to showcase his new mill technology. Furthermore, the local merchant class was opposed to his exclusive patents so it was also a chance to demonstrate the efficiency of his new manufacturing system (Miller and Glithero, 2016, 98–99).

Excavations in 2005 and 2014–2015 showed Arkwright's Shudehill mill was 66 metres long, 9.1 metres wide and five storeys high. The wooden floors were supported by a central row of cast-iron columns on each floor. There was an internal, centrally placed wheel pit. His attempt in 1781–82 to run the textile machinery directly using steam power generated by an atmospheric engine, manufactured by the London-based Thomas Hunt, proved unsuccessful. No archaeological evidence survived for this experimental set-up. Remains associated with the installation of the replacement returning engine installed in 1783 were found. This followed the same

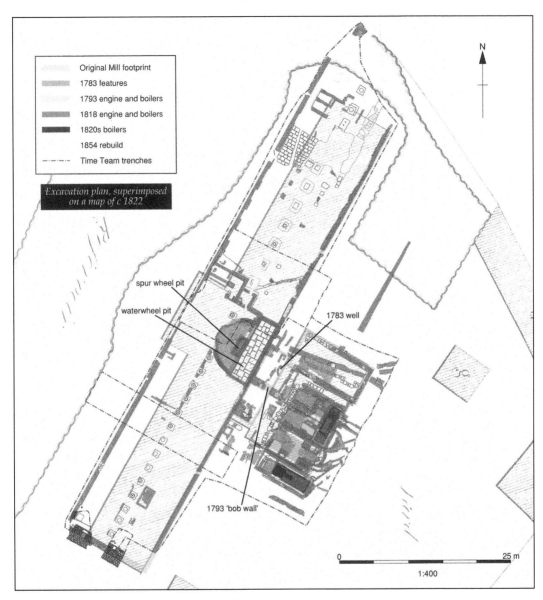

Arkwright's mill was first excavated in 2005 and then in 2014 to 2015 the whole site was tripped and recorded, ahead of redevelopment by the Co-Operative Wholesale Society, by Oxford Archaeology North. (Image courtesy of Oxford Archaeology North)

principle Arkwright employed at his Wirksworth Mill (though on a larger scale), where a steam engine pumped water from a well fed by a reservoir directly onto a waterwheel that ran the textile machinery. At Shudehill the remains of the beam wall and a well placed between the engine cylinder and the pump barrel suggested this new arrangement comprised a 30-inch (0.76-metre) steam cylinder and two probably 20-inch (0.5-metre) pumps which fed an 18-foot (5.48-metres) diameter waterwheel.

The wheelpit was found to be largely intact during the excavations. The engine ran continuously, consuming 70 cwt (3.56 tons) of coal per day. The chimney used to vent the waste gases from the adjacent boiler became a noted Manchester landmark in the 1780s (Miller and Glithero, 2016, 101–12).

Once Arkwright's Shudehill Mill had been built, Manchester's industrialization took off with the construction of thirty-three water and steam-powered textile mills during the 1780s and 1790s. This mill-building boom turned a regional manufacturing town into the world's first industrial city based around the mass manufacturing of cotton thread. By 1800 at least nineteen textile mill sites in the city were using steam power to supplement or run directly cotton spinning machinery. The high technical capital cost was offset by building large multi-storeyed manufacturing units using the latest technology to increase the rate of production to spin high-value yarn products (Nevell, 2018, 16–19). Arkwright's Shudehill Mill pioneered this new form of factory-based manufacture within the city and the wider Lancashire cotton industry.

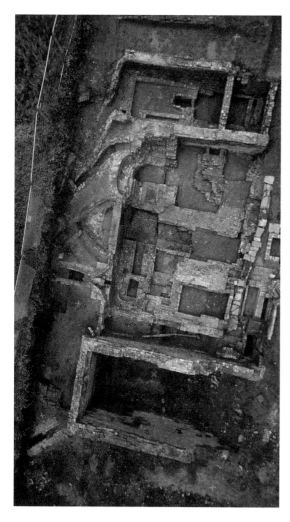

An aerial view of the late eighteenth and early nineteenth-century boiler and engine houses at Arkwright's Shudehill Mill, as excavated in 2014–15. (Image courtesy of Oxford Archaeology North)

Dig 19

Dying in Industrial Manchester – The Cross Street Chapel Graveyard (2014–2015)

The excavation of workers' housing can reveal extensive evidence for the state of sanitation in the domestic properties of industrial Manchester, and by implication the quality of living conditions and the likelihood of disease. Until recently this fieldwork and contemporary accounts of health and disease from the Victorian city were the only sources of evidence for the living conditions of industrial Manchester. This changed

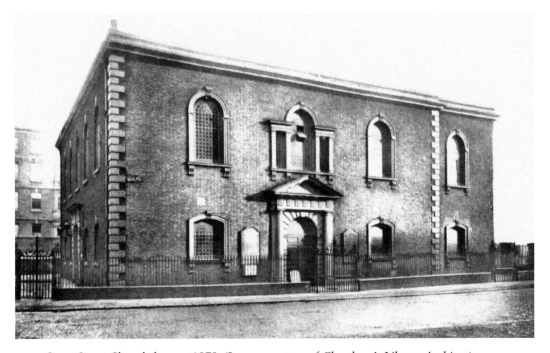

Cross Street Chapel, from *c*. 1879. (Image courtesy of Cheetham's Library Archives)

when, between September 2014 and November 2015, 241 bodies were excavated and exhumed from the graveyard of Cross Street Chapel, in central Manchester. The bodies spanned the early eighteenth century to the middle of the nineteenth century. This was the first time such a large group of human remains from Manchester's Georgian and Victorian periods had been scientifically studied, and the analysis of the skeletons gives a glimpse into the living conditions of the industrial city at its height.

The excavation work was carried out in advance of the construction of the Manchester Metrolink and was commissioned by Transport for Greater Manchester (TfGM) and undertaken by CFA Archaeology Limited. The archaeological excavation took place along the frontage of Cross Street Chapel, in a narrow strip no more than 5 metres wide, 34 metres long and in places more than 3 metres deep. The site was covered in a large portable tent throughout the dig, which became an unusual feature of central Manchester. The skeletons were analysed by York Osteoarchaeology in 2016 and reinterred at Manchester Southern Cemetery in January 2017 (CFA, 2017, 1–12).

The purpose-built Cross Street Chapel opened as a dissenters' meeting house in 1694 and became an important focus for the religious and political history of Manchester (Kidd & Wyke, 2016, 180–181). It was destroyed and rebuilt on several occasions, notably in 1715 and 1940, the present building dating from 1995–97 (Hartwell, Hyde & Pevsner, 2015, 312). The excavations located the southern road frontage of

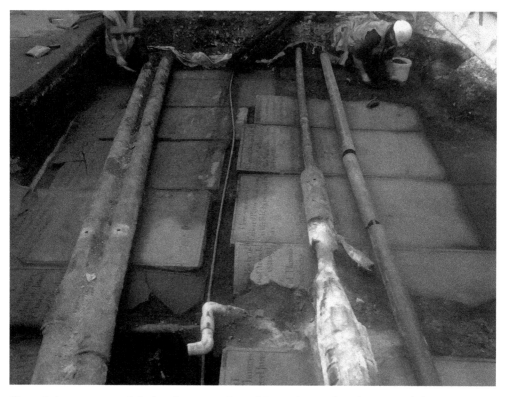

Grave ledgers uncovered during the excavation of Cross Street Chapel graveyard during 2014 by CFA Archaeology. (Image courtesy of the Greater Manchester Archaeological Advisory Service)

the 1690s and eighteenth-century chapel, which was brick-built and ran for 25 metres. It also located part of the western boundary wall of the churchyard. The surrounding graveyard was divided into a lower and upper burial ground, the upper section being on the eastern side of the chapel on higher ground. Three phases of road widening on Cross Street in 1845, 1871 and 1897 brought an end to the active use of the graveyard. By the end of the century it was completely hidden under the road and pavements (CFA, 2017, 6–7).

The skeletons were found in both wooden and lead coffins in family grave plots, or 'stacks', that were marked with gravestones depicting the names, ages and dates of death of the individuals below. From the gravestone information and other corroborative historical information, from various written sources and burial artefacts, it was possible to successfully identify 172 skeletons as named individuals. In addition to these skeletons, over 17,000 disarticulated bones were recorded, testifying to the high frequency of use of the graveyard (CFA, 2017, 22–23).

The population represented the middle ranks of Manchester's Georgian and early Victorian society. It has been observed that the majority of those who attended Cross Street Chapel were of the professional and skilled members of society, those that ran

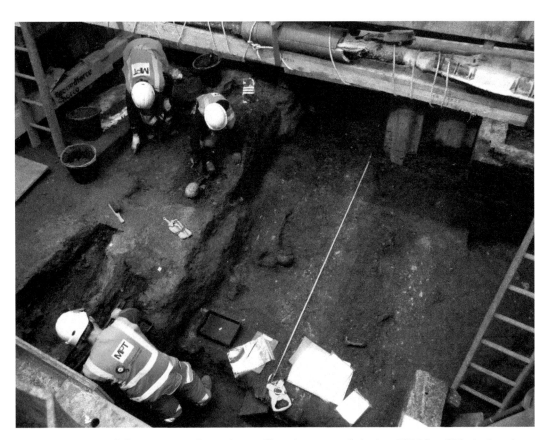

Excavation of the graves at Cross Street Chapel graveyard during 2015 by CFA Archaeology. (Image courtesy of the Greater Manchester Archaeological Advisory Service)

manufactories and local businesses, but it also included some of the skilled working class (Kidd & Wyke, 2016, 180).

The skeletons varied considerably in their completeness and state of preservation. Most were largely complete, with only moderate fragmentation, and were in a moderate to good state of preservation. A number of children and adolescents were found to suffer from nutritional deficiencies, with evidence for rickets and scurvy common. A number of the adult skeletons showed evidence for activity-related skeletal pathology. Numerous mild congenital anomalies were noted on many of the adult skeletons, particularly within the spine. Traumatic injuries were frequently observed, particularly in males. The most frequent types of injury included fractured bones which had healed prior to death.

Evidence of diseases affecting the lungs, such as pneumonia or tuberculosis, was identified in 8 per cent of the adults (particularly males). A number of individuals, including adults and non-adults, had suffered from inflammatory lesions on the inside of the skull, which could have been due to a number of causes, including meningitis, scurvy, rickets, tuberculosis or cranial trauma. Levels of non-specific infection were double the levels recorded for the post-medieval period, with males being more frequently affected in the lower limbs and females and non-adults more commonly affected in the upper limbs. The dental health of the population was worse than the post-medieval average, and the high frequency of tooth decay and the pattern of cavity location were both consistent with a diet high in sugar and refined carbohydrates (CFA, 2017, 22–23).

In addition to the skeletons, the excavation recovered a variety of other objects, from the coffins and their plaques, jewellery such as finger rings, and grave textiles, to clay pipes and 282 sherds of pottery (largely background noise from previous activity along Cross Street). In one case floral remains of rosemary leaves were identified in the remains of an infant's wooden coffin.

The Cross Street Chapel bodies provide a first glimpse into the physical consequences of living in the dynamic industrial city that Manchester was becoming in the later eighteenth and early nineteenth century. Generalisations from such a small sample are always dangerous, especially as Manchester's population in 1841, just a few years before the cemetery went out of use, was over 235,000, whilst only 241 skeletons were investigated at Cross Street. However, this project demonstrates one of archaeology's greatest strengths: the ability to bring the present into personal contact with the past through the physical remains of our ancestors.

In the last forty years, since the establishment of the first professional archaeologists based within the city, it has been possible to recover the story of Manchester's ordinary folk, the people who tilled the crops, built the roads and ran the factories, in ever more detail. This archaeological work enables us to commemorate and celebrate their contribution in the creation of the twenty-first-century, vibrant, diverse, and outward-looking City of Manchester.

Dig 20

Digging The Reno, Hulme (2017)

The excavation of the Reno nightclub, a key part of Manchester's late twentieth-century music scene, was in many ways the culmination of nearly two decades of community and professional archaeological research within the city. The idea of exploring through a community archaeology excavation the site of a late twentieth-century music venue, with this initiative coming from within the local Afro-Caribbean community, who would excavate their own past in their own lifetime, would have been unthinkable without the Dig Manchester and Dig Greater Manchester projects and forty years of professional urban archaeology experience.

The 'Excavating The Reno' project brought together oral history and archaeology in a three-week excavation in October 2017, exploring the story of a Manchester soul and funk club that became a welcoming sanctuary from the racism that mixed-heritage members of the local community often experienced in the 1970s. Some of the original DJs and dancers from the 1970s and early 1980s returned to help excavate the converted basement that housed the club, recovering an array of finds from vinyl records to flared trousers, and capturing the memories of many club goers (Nevell & Cattell, 2018, 40–41).

Located in Hulme, on the outskirts of the city, the Reno occupied the basement of a large Edwardian building on Princess Road, one of the main routes into Manchester city centre. It was originally filled by shops with residential flats above, but in the mid-1950s the structure was converted into an African Seamen's Mission. It soon became a meeting place for Manchester's fledgling African and Caribbean communities. Informal drinking and gambling clubs sprang up within its walls, and it was these groups that eventually led to the opening of several pubs and clubs in the building during the 1960s and 1970s. Soon the area was hugely popular with the local community as somewhere new and exotic to spend a night out, and the Reno in particular was renowned for its music.

Throughout the 1970s and 1980s, the club was celebrated for its rare funk and soul music – sometimes it was the only place in the country playing certain records, which were imported by long-standing DJ Persian – as well as for its late licence, with many nights out in town finishing there in the early hours. Although rather dingy, the thriving club was visited by celebrities including Muhammad Ali, while the snooker star Alex Higgins was a regular, and record producer Tony Wilson had his stag do there. It was more than that to the local community: to those who went there every weekend, in some cases every night, it was a haven from the disapproval and prejudice they encountered in their daily lives (Nevell & Cattell, 2018).

By the time the Reno closed in 1986, Hulme and Moss Side, with its large African, Asian and Caribbean communities, had suffered years of high unemployment and unrest, including rioting in 1981. Local playwright Linda Brogan, who visited the Reno in the 1970s when aged just sixteen, had for years been thinking about new ways to tell the story of the club and get the club community back together. Inspired by the Dig Greater Manchester project, she hit upon the idea of physically going back into the Reno by digging it up. She approached Salford Archaeology at the University of Salford with a plan to resurrect the club through archaeology, art and film. Linda was also keen to tell

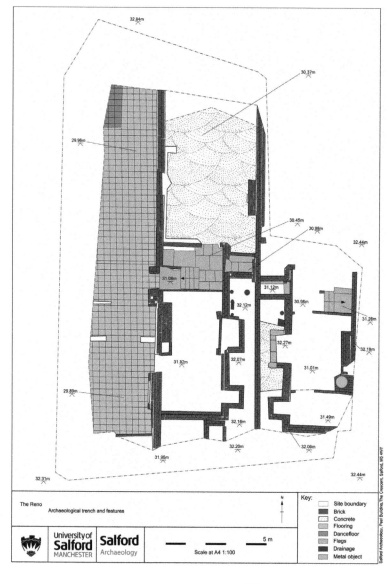

An excavated plan of the late nineteenth-century basement used as The Reno nightclub in the 1970s and early 1980s in Hulme, Manchester.

the story of Hulme and Moss Side's mixed-heritage community to a wider audience, while simultaneously proving to that community that despite years of being overlooked, their story was valid and relevant and needed to be heard. For Linda Brogan one of the most important aspects of the excavation was getting the Reno regulars to volunteer alongside professional and volunteer archaeologists and encouraging the interaction between the two groups in their pursuit of a common goal. She wanted the project to break down the racial and class barriers that the regulars had been faced with for so long, one of the problems identified during the Dig Greater Manchester project (Nevell, 2019, 87), and, as happened in the Dig Greater Manchester project, to get them working with people they would not normally come across in their ordinary lives (Coen, Meredith & Condie, 2017).

The Reno's footprint filled the full 17-metre width of the basement, which survived to ceiling height, with the bar, dance floor and toilets at the front, and a kitchen and a smaller room for gambling at the back. The excavations uncovered the back stairs on the eastern side of the building that had once led up to the ground floor, as well as the alleyway and cellars to the rear of the property beyond the stairs. Although not physically part of the Reno itself, the alley was an important element of the story, as it was the quickest way out during the not-uncommon police raids on the venue. Indeed, many of the project's more interesting finds, including clothing, make-up, wallets and drinks bottles, were found in the grids and cellar lights of this passageway.

As more and more of the club was uncovered, there was constant debate raging between the regulars as to what they were looking at. This was a new experience for the professional archaeologists onsite, led by Sarah Cattell, who had never had so many 'consultants' onsite before who knew the structures that they were excavating so well, and who of whom the archaeologists could ask about finer details such as internal decor. Photographs and memories from the club indicated the two front rooms on the western side of the building, the dance floor and kitchen, had wood-effect panelling on the walls and red and blue lino tiles on the floor, with an area of red tiles for the dance floor. Although the floor was well preserved, all that remained of the panelling was plastic corner trims and occasional fragments of hardboard, but this absence allowed the archaeologists to see that the wall behind was constructed from white glazed brick.

The Reno project was led by the local Afro-Caribbean community and many of the volunteers on the dig were past club visitors.

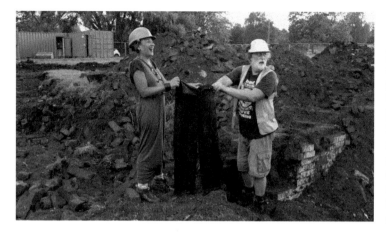

Late twentieth-century objects recovered from the dig by the University of Salford included a pair of 1970s flared jeans, shown here with local artist Linda Brogan, the inspiration and driving force behind the dig, and one of the dig volunteers.

This reflected the building's earlier incarnation: it was a common feature of Edwardian basement rooms, which were often originally used as kitchens, laundries and cold-storage spaces. The glazed bricks extended the full length of the club and included curved examples around the doorways, which still retained fragments of their wooden frames in places. It was in one of these that another of the more memorable finds was made: a pair of green nylon ladies' flares, in near-perfect condition (Nevell & Cattell, 2018, 43–44).

The rooms to the rear of the club were more conservatively decorated, with the kitchen retaining its blue painted bricks, again common for cellars in this type of building – a shade referred to by the club regulars, who immediately recognised it, as 'Reno blue'. The

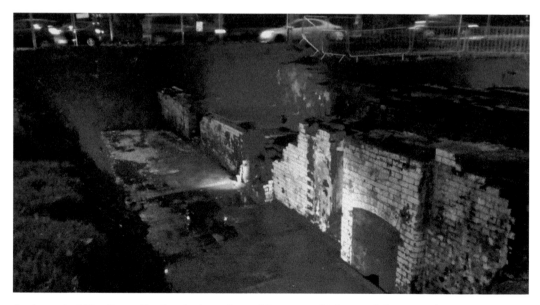

At the end of The Reno dig, the site hosted a public event which saw club music played on site for the first time since the 1980s and the excavated dance floor/basement lit up as part of the celebrations.

gambling room to the north had plastered and painted walls, and a concrete floor that, where it had been broken, revealed a laid-brick surface underneath. The room also had a small fireplace, complete with its 1970s-style grate and fret. This feature was remembered well by the regulars, who recalled frustrated gamblers throwing their dice into it when they lost, and the stifling heat of the room, especially in the summer, as the fire was always lit whatever the weather. Fittingly, several dice were found in this room, along with drinks bottles and pieces of Formica tabletops (Nevell & Cattell, 2018, 44–45).

The 'Excavating The Reno' project's story has continued to evolve since the dig ended, driven by the local community. Linda Brogan, the artist behind the inspiration for the project, secured a residency at the Whitworth Art Gallery in Manchester during 2019 and 2020, where she has collected ideas, material and volunteers to create an innovative and interactive exhibition about the Reno and its community. The Reno experience demonstrates the way in which archaeological analysis, whether through excavation or recording standing building remains, provides a unique form of data that is not available through any other discipline. That is true whether those remains are that of a prehistoric farmstead, Roman fort, medieval rubbish pit, or when dealing with the archaeology of the twentieth century, for which there is a plethora of other sources.

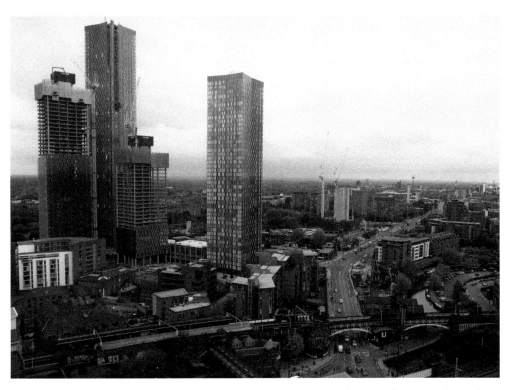

The Castlefield area, looking south along Chester Road, showing the new skyscrapers being built on the site of Roman and industrial Manchester during 2019. The economic development of Manchester in the early twenty-first century continues to provide threats and opportunities for the city's nationally important archaeology and heritage. (Image courtesy of the Greater Manchester Archaeological Advisory Service)

Acknowledgements

I would like to thank the following people and organisations who have helped to explore Manchester's archaeology over the last forty years: the staff of Salford Archaeology, based at the University of Salford and ably led by Adam Thompson, and the former staff of the University of Manchester Archaeological Unit (UMAU), especially Dr Peter Arrowsmith and David Power; the staff of Manchester Museum and the Museum of Science and Industry in Manchester; as well as the many other archaeological contractors who have worked to uncover, understand and protect the city's archaeological past over the last decade. I would also like to thank Norman Redhead of the Greater Manchester Archaeological Advisory Service (GMAAS), for his help in choosing the twenty 'best' digs in the city, and his tireless promotion of the city's archaeology; Adam Thompson, director of Salford Archaeology, for his support, ideas and encouragement over many years; Dr Andy Myers of GMAAS for his advice and knowledge on all things prehistoric; and Prof John Walker, formerly deputy director of the Greater Manchester Archaeological Unit, and the first director of UMAU, for tea and sympathy over many years. Copyright permission for specific images is given in the relevant captions. Finally, thanks to Catherine Mackey, who provided assistance with editing the final text.

About the Author

Dr Michael Nevell, DPhil, MCIfA, FSA, is a landscape archaeologist with more than thirty years' experience. His research interests include the archaeology of industrialization, community archaeology, and historic buildings, especially textile mills, timber buildings, and weavers' cottages. Dr Nevell has written extensively on the archaeology and historic landscape of the Manchester city region and has been a senior lecturer in archaeology at both the University of Manchester and University of Salford. He was director of the University of Manchester Archaeological Unit from 2002 to 2009 and founding Head of the Centre for Applied Archaeology at the University of Salford from 2009 to 2020. You can follow him on twitter @archaeology_tea or read his blog: www.archaeologytea.wordpress.com

Bibliography

A number of excavations discussed in this book are published as free-to-download booklets in the Greater Manchester's Past Revealed series, and are available from: diggreatermanchester.wordpress.com.

Askew, S., S. Bell, A. Thompson, P. Wilson & M. Nevell, 2009, 'Whitecarr Lane, Hale, Trafford: An Archaeological Excavation of a 14th and 15th Century Bloomery Furnace Site.' University of Manchester unpublished client report.

Axon, W. E. A., 1886, *Annals of Manchester*.

Bell, S., 2009, *Dig Manchester: Northenden Mill Community Excavations 2005 to 2006*. Manchester: University of Manchester Archaeological Unit.

Bone, P. W., 2005, 'A Survey of the Glass Industry in Manchester and Salford 1800–1967.' Unpublished MA thesis, the Ironbridge Institute, University of Birmingham.

Brennand, M., with G. Chitty & M. Nevell, 2006, *The Archaeology of North West England. An Archaeological Research Framework for North west England: Volume 1. Resource Assessment*. Archaeology North West Volume 8.

Bruton, F. A., (ed.), 1909, *The Roman Fort at Manchester*. Manchester University Press.

Bruton, F. A. & J. P. Hall (eds), 1923, *Caer Llugwy. Excavation of the Roman fort between Capel Curig and Bettws-y-Coed. First Report*. Manchester: Taylor & Garnett Evans.

Cattell, S. & M. Nevell, 2011, 'The Workers' Housing on vacant land on the corner of Pickford Street and Jersey Street: an archaeological excavation.' Centre for Applied Archaeology: Unpublished client report.

CFA, 2017, 'Cross Street Chapel Manchester. Archaeological Excavation and Exhumation Assessment report.' Stockport: CFA Archaeology Ltd unpublished client report.

Champness, B. & M. Nevell, 2003, 'A Note on the Archaeology of Manchester's Glass Industry', *Industrial Archaeology North West*, Volume 1.3 (Issue 3), 22–4.

Coen S., J. Meredith & J. Condie, 2017, 'I Dig Therefore We Are: Community Archaeology, Place-based Social Identity, and Intergroup Relations within Local Communities', *Journal of Community & Applied Social Psychology* 27.3, 212–225.

Day, J. & Tylecote R. (eds), 1991, *The Industrial Revolution in Metals*. London: Institute of Metals.

Dodgson, J. McN., 1970, *The Place-Names of Cheshire Part I*. English Place-Name Society 44 (for 1966–7).

Earwaker, J. P. 1877. *East Cheshire: Past and Present vol I*.

Garner, D. J., 2007, *The Neolithic and Bronze Age Settlement at Oversley Farm, Styal, Cheshire. Excavations in advance of Manchester Airport's Second Runway, 1997–8.* Gifford Archaeological Monographs Number One, Oxford.

Garratt, R., 2009, *Dig Manchester, Moston Hall. Community Excavations 2003 to 2005.* Manchester: University of Manchester Archaeological Unit.

GMAU, 1981, *Greater Manchester Archaeological Unit Annual Report 1980–81.* Manchester University.

Graham, J. A. & B. A. Phythian, 1965, *The Manchester Grammar School 1515–1965.* Manchester University Press.

Gregory, R. A., 2005, 'Hardman Street Soda works, Deansgate, Manchester.' Unpublished UMAU Report 2005.

Gregory, R. A., 2007a, *Roman Manchester: The University of Manchester's Excavations within the Vicus 2001–5.* Oxford. Oxbow Monographs.

Gregory, R. A., 2007b, 'The Late Professor G D B Jones' Deansgate Excavations 1977–78. An Archive Report.' Unpublished research report for GMAU.

Gregory, R. A., 2007c, 'Loom Street, Ancoats, Manchester. An Archaeological Excavation of Late Eighteenth and Nineteenth Century Workers' Housing.' Unpublished UMAU Report 2007.

Gregory, R. A., 2008, 'Peel Hall, Wythenshawe, Manchester. An Archaeological Evaluation.' University of Manchester Archaeological Unit unpublished client report.

Gregory, R. A., 2019, *Greater Manchester's Past Revealed 24. Cutacre. Excavating a Prehistoric, Medieval and Post-medieval Landscape.* Lancaster: Oxford Archaeology North.

Griffiths, D., 2001, 'The North-West Frontier', in N. J. Higham & D. H. Hill (eds), 2001, *Edward the Elder: 899-924.* London, Routledge, 167–87.

Groves, J., 1994, *Piggin, Husslements, and Desperate Debts: a social history of North-east Cheshire, through wills and probate inventories, 1600-1760.* Sale: Northern Writers Advisory Service.

Hartwell, C., M. Hyde & N. Pevsner, 2004, *The Buildings of England. Lancashire: Manchester the South-East.* London: Yale University Press.

Hayes, L., 2014, *Greater Manchester's Past Revealed 11. Iron & Steel in Openshaw: Excavating John Ashbury's Carriage and Iron Works.* Aylesbury: PCA.

Jones, G. D. B., 1984, *Past Imperfect. A History of Rescue Archaeology.* Phillimore, Chichester.

Jones G. D. B. & S. Grealey, 1974, *Roman Manchester.* Altrincham.

Jones G. D. B. & D. Mattingly, 1990, *An Atlas of Roman Britain.* Oxford: Blackwell.

Jones G.D.B. & P. Reynolds, 1978, *The Deansgate Excavations 1987 – an interim report.* Greater Manchester Council, Greater Manchester Archaeological Group, Manchester Museum & Dept of Archaeology, University of Manchester.

Kidd, A. & T. Wyke (eds), 2016, *Manchester. Making the Modern City.* Liverpool University Press.

Miller, I., 2007, 'Percival, Vickers & Co Ltd, Ancoats: The Archaeology of a Nineteenth Century-Century Manchester Flint Glassworks', *Industrial Archaeology Review* 29.1, 13–29.

Miller, I. & O. Cook, 2019, *Greater Manchester's Past Revealed 25. Deansgate Square, Manchester: Archaeology Beyond the Medlock.* Salford: Salford Archaeology within the University of Salford.

Miller, I. & Glithero J., 2016, 'Richard Arkwright's Shudehill Mill: The Archaeology of Manchester's First Steampowered Cotton Mill', *Industrial Archaeology Review* 38.2: 98–118.

Miller, I. & C. Wild, 2015, *Greater Manchester's Past Revealed 14. 'Hell Upon Earth'. The Archaeology of Angel Meadow*. Lancaster: Oxford Archaeology North.

Morris, M. (ed.), 1983, *Medieval Manchester: A Regional Study. The Archaeology of Greater Manchester volume 1*.

Murphy, P., 2015, 'Building a Head of Steam: Digging Moston', in M. Nevell & N. Redhead, 2015, *Archaeology for All: Community Archaeology in the early 21st Century*. University of Salford, 89–94.

Nevell, M., 2008, *Manchester: The Hidden History*. Stroud: The History Press.

Nevell, M., 2010, 'Excavating the Cotton Mill. Towards a Research Framework for the Below-Ground Remains of the Textile Industry', in P. Belford, M. Palmer & R. White, *Footprints of Industry. Papers from the 300th anniversary conference at Coalbrookdale, 3-7 June 2009*. BAR British Series 523, 153–68.

Nevell, M., 2013, 'Archaeology for All: managing expectations and learning from the past for the future – the Dig Manchester community archaeology experience', in C. Dalglish (ed.), *Archaeology, the Public and Recent Past*. The Boydell Press.

Nevell, M., 2014, 'Legislation and Reality: The Archaeological Evidence for Sanitation and Housing Quality in Urban Workers' Housing in the Ancoats Area of Manchester Between 1800 and 1950.' *Industrial Archaeology Review* 36.1: 48–74.

Nevell, M., 2017, 'More than Just Digging the Map – Excavating and Recording Workers' Housing', *Industrial Archaeology Review* 39.2, 83–84.

Nevell, M., 2018, *Manchester at Work*. Stroud: Amberley Publishing.

Nevell, M., 2019a, 'Saving Manchester's Industrial Past: Regeneration and New Uses of Industrial Archaeology Structures in Greater Manchester, 1980 to 2018', *Transactions of the Lancashire & Cheshire Antiquarian Society* vol. 111, 99–117.

Nevell, M., 2019b, 'The Dig Greater Manchester Community Project, 2011 to 2017: Archaoelogy for All?', *Memoirs of the Manchester Literary & Philosophical Association* Volume 156, 77–89.

Nevell, M., 2019c, 'Excavating Peterloo and the Manchester 'Spring'', *Current Archaeology* Issue 357 (December), 34–40.

Nevell, M. & S. Cattell, 2018, 'Resurrecting the Reno: Unearthing the soul of a boundary-pushing Manchester club', *Current Archaeology* Issue 342 (September), 40–45.

Nevell, M. with B. Grimsditch & I. Hradil, 2007, *The Archaeology of Tameside Volume 7: Denton and the Archaeology of the Felt Hatting Industry*. Tameside MBC and UMAU.

Parkinson-Bailey, J. J., 2000, *Manchester. An Architectural History*. Manchester University Press.

PCA, 2009, 'An Archaeological Excavation at Chester Road/Great Jackson Street Excavation, Manchester, Greater Manchester.' Durham: PCA unpublished client report.

Poole S., 2012, 'What don't we know about Peterloo?', in *Return to Peterloo, Manchester Region History Review* Volume 23, 1–18.

Redhead, N., 1996, 'Medieval Furnaces in the Castleshaw Valley', *Archaeology North West* Vol 2.4 (Issue No. 10), 99–104.

Redhead, N., 2004, 'The Archaeology of South-East Lancashire', in Hartwell, Hyde & Pevsner, 2004, 11–23.

Roeder, C., 1899, 'Recent Roman discoveries in Deansgate and on Hunt's bank and Roman Manchester restudied', in *Transactions of the Lancashire & Cheshire Antiquarian Society* vol. 17.

Thompson, A., 2015, 'Dig Greater Manchester: Accessing, Exploring and Celebrating Local Archaeology', in M. Nevell & N. Redhead, 2015, *Archaeology for All: Community Archaeology in the early 21st Century*. University of Salford, 151–158.

Walker, J. S. F. (ed.), 1986, *Roman Manchester: A Frontier Settlement. The Archaeology of Greater Manchester volume 3*.

Walker, J. S. F. (ed.), 1989, *Castleshaw - The Archaeology of a Roman Fortlet. The Archaeology of Greater Manchester volume 4*. Greater Manchester Archaeological Unit.

Walker, J. S. F. & A. S. Tindall (eds), 1985, *Country Houses of Greater Manchester. The Archaeology of Greater Manchester, vol. 2*. Greater Manchester Archaeological Unit.

Whitaker, J., 1773, *History of Manchester volume 2*. Manchester.

Williams, M. with D. Farnie, 1992, *Cotton Mills in Greater Manchester*. The Greater Manchester Archaeological Unit in association with the Royal Commission on the Historical Monuments of England, Carnegie Publishing Ltd, Preston.